Son of the Vikings, the Sequel

"… and He Shares His Father's Faith"

By Glenn F. Engen, Ph.D.

With Aletha Gruzensky

TEACH Services, Inc.
P U B L I S H I N G

www.TEACHServices.com • (800) 367-1844

Copyright © 2023 Glenn F. Engen
Copyright © 2023 TEACH Services, Inc.
ISBN-13: 978-1-4796-1553-7 (Paperback)
ISBN-13: 978-1-4796-1554-4 (ePub)
Library of Congress Control Number: 2023905579

All Scripture quotations, unless otherwise indicated, are taken from the King James Version®. Public domain.

Published by

TEACH Services, Inc.
P U B L I S H I N G
www.TEACHServices.com ● (800) 367-1844

Dedication

Dedicated to the memory of Dr. Burgess R. Bills MD, who, while a pre-med student, was there for me as an understanding, supportive, and nonjudgmental friend when I was in a difficult situation and whose support "made the difference."

And in memory of my beloved first wife, Sadie Owen Engen, my companion for fifty-six years, whose loving support carried me through the events related in this story.

Table of Contents

Preface

Glenn F. Engen is a well-published author in the technical field of microwave metrology. However, the language of scientific papers differs from that of storytelling. For this reason, one day Glenn handed me a manila envelope with this story and asked if I would be willing to read it and assist him with it. His first wife Sadie had started to help him put in details that would make it more story-like, but she had passed away. I took the story home and read through it.

I have known Glenn and Sadie Engen since I was eight years old, after my family moved to Boulder, Colorado. Sadie was a favorite substitute teacher in the school I attended. Later I took a year out of college to work with a writing group of which Sadie was a part. This group co-authored the *Ladder of Life* series of books for preschool children. As I read through Glenn's story, I could spot the details Sadie had added. I left these in the story.

Since I had grown up in Boulder and my father had also worked at the National Bureau of Standards where Glenn worked, I knew many of the events, locations, and people in the story. I have tried to keep Glenn's flavor and his manner of speech while adding some details to help the reader visualize the events. I have also changed some narrative paragraphs into conversations and changed scientific passive verbs to active verbs to keep the story moving. As Glenn and I have worked on this, more of the story and more details have come out. These have made the story better.

It is my hope that in reading this incredible story, people might be drawn closer to God who works through events to write stories in people's lives. My own heart has found encouragement—and patience—in realizing that some stories require generations to reach a conclusion.

—Aletha Gruzensky

Acknowledgements

I want to acknowledge Josephine Cunnington Edwards for writing the book *Son of the Vikings* about my father's experience and for preaching his funeral service. Without her, this stream of highly unlikely, indeed providential events, would never have occurred.

Thank you to many friends for their support through difficult times. Although some are mentioned in the story, many more have played a part in the events as they unfolded. Thank you to all.

I also want to thank my wife Bona for her support as I reach back into the past to tell a story about my first wife Sadie.

Prologue

"Denmark. We are actually on our way," my wife Sadie remarked as we settled into our airline seats.

"It seems impossible after all that's happened in the last few days," I replied. "But yes, we are going to the land of my father's birth, where his relatives still live." Although we had gone across the Atlantic on a number of occasions, never before had the trip been undertaken with such a combination of prior events, mixed feelings, or apprehension as to how it would unfold.

Somewhere over the North Atlantic and at an altitude of perhaps 38,000 feet, we ate dinner and the stewardess picked up the trays. The last rays of the setting sun bid farewell to the soft, billowy clouds which partially obscured my view of the bright blue ocean below. In the cabin, some awaited the beginning of the promised feature movie. Others, like Sadie and me, attempted to find a comfortable position and settle down for what would be a short night. But before closing my eyes, I paused to reflect upon the events of the past few days and order my thoughts for the days to come.

Let's see, I have the tape, the tape recorder, and fresh batteries. But Father, my thoughts continued and became a prayer, *the folk with whom I want to share these words on tape have a very limited understanding of English, and I certainly have no knowledge of Danish. But then, if You want to rearrange the electronics inside that recorder in such a way that the English recorded on the tape is converted into Danish before it emerges from the loudspeaker, that will be a trivial thing in comparison to what You've already done. For once I refuse to worry about it. Not that You expect me to. This whole trip was Your idea. It certainly wasn't mine, although I'm certainly happy to be making it....*

Chapter 1

S ome months earlier, I'd gone to work as usual, not knowing that this day would mark the start of a new adventure with God. All seemed the same—the crisp high-altitude air, the azure blue Colorado sky, and the flat grey buildings of the Boulder Laboratories of the National Bureau of Standards[1] (NBS) where I'd worked for more than two decades as part of the microwave staff.

My uncle had introduced me to radio when I was a ten-year-old lad. He had taken a spool of insulated wire, wound it around a discarded oatmeal container, and provided a few other things he had, of which the galena crystal was most important. With the help of a "cat whisker" (a piece of wire), I succeeded in finding a "sensitive spot" on the crystal and was rewarded by hearing the "half-million-watt voice of the nation's station, WLW Cincinnati," over 100 miles from our home in North Carolina. I remembered the delight I felt.

> *Some months earlier, I'd gone to work as usual, not knowing that this day would mark the start of a new adventure with God.*

From this simple beginning, I continued to build radios. First, I built a one-tube radio. Instead of the huge and expensive "B battery" usually used, I used flashlight batteries—ones I could afford. Next, I constructed a 110-volt AC-DC, five-tube, superheterodyne radio. Some years later, while attending Emmanuel Missionary College (EMC), I learned and passed the Morris code exam and the theory exam to become a licensed radio amateur. I helped build an amateur radio station for the college. Each experience brought me closer to my current job with the NBS.

I continued walking toward the front door of the NBS laboratories, looking up at the Flatirons, huge monoliths for which Boulder is famous. Behind the Flatirons foothills, the Rocky Mountains reached upward to over 14,000 feet. To the east, the Great Plains stretched far into Nebraska and Kansas, the flat horizon broken only by buildings and an occasional mesa or butte. As I walked, absorbing another of Colorado's many sunny days, I silently thanked God that I had the chance to live in Boulder instead of Tacoma Park, Maryland, where I'd been working when I started dating my wife, Sadie.

---

1   This government agency is now the National Institute of Science and Technology.

Sadie had come to Tacoma Park for a few months to work on a temporary book project. We'd known each other in college. In fact, I had attempted to date her a time or two but lost interest when it ended up as a double date—*she with a different boy of her choice* and I "stuck" with one of her girlfriends who for unknown reasons apparently had an interest in me.

That had been five years prior. My current romantic interests were elsewhere but had stalled. However, I had "wheels" and invited Sadie and her girlfriend to go to a US Armed Forces band concert in downtown Washington, D.C. Sadie reluctantly accepted but also made sure that an additional girlfriend came, and I found myself with a "harem." After that, the concert trips continued—minus the attendants.

The summer passed, but the seed of love had been planted. When Sadie left a few months later, I made numerous trips back to Michigan where she taught school. We got married the next summer and she moved to Tacoma Park, where I worked at the Johns Hopkins Applied Physics Laboratory. However, Sadie and I weren't completely comfortable in that environment.

Then I heard about a job possibility with the National Bureau of Standards. As suggested by its name, the National Bureau of Standards (NBS) functions as the final authority in the United States for the length of an inch, the weight[2] of a pound, and for the time of day. Electrical energy is bought and sold by the kilowatt hour. Obviously, both the utility company and the consumer have substantial interest in having the meter reading correct. The NBS develops and maintains the methods for confirming this accuracy. The distance at which radar can recognize an airplane depends, in part, upon the amount of micro-wave power which the radar is able to generate. The same is true of the speed with which a microwave oven operates. The NBS develops methods for evaluating the accuracy of the meters which measure this power.

Initially, all of the NBS functions were located in central Washington, D.C. The threat of nuclear warfare, prevalent at the time, led to a high-level decision to decentralize some parts of government agencies away from Washington. Colorado's diverse terrain offered certain advantages for the work of the Central Radio Propagation Laboratory.

"Sadie," I said, "Here's an interesting possibility. The Central Radio Propagation Laboratory, part of the National Bureau of Standards, will be moving to Boulder, Colorado. Should we consider that as a possible place to live?"

"I've never been to Colorado."

---

2   More correctly, the *mass* of a pound.

"Neither have I. Maybe we could go take a look. I can take some vacation time."

"That's a good idea, Glenn. I'll pack the car, so when you get home from work, we can start."

True to her promise, Sadie had the car ready to go at 5:30 p.m. on the appointed day. I climbed in and started driving, while Sadie started unpacking the lunch she had prepared for supper. She handed me food items while I drove. After a few hours we switched drivers and as night came on, we alternated between driving and curling up on the backseat to get some sleep. For twenty-four hours, we stopped only for fuel or to change drivers. After a brief overnight stop, we arrived in Boulder on the second day, having driven 1,800 miles. Although we were only in Boulder for two days, it was long enough to convince us that this was the place we would like to live.

My next challenge was to obtain a position with the soon-to-depart National Bureau of Standards. Many of its staff had elected to find other employment in the Washington, D.C. area rather than move with their agency. This left many vacancies. I applied and got an interview.

"I'm sorry, but we aren't interested in any misfits." With these words my interview was about to close when I protested, "But if you will please check my references, I think you will find that I am neither a misfit nor incompetent."

"Well, we'll think it over," the interviewer replied without making a commitment.

Chapter 2

For a week or more I anxiously awaited a further response but apparently it was not to be forthcoming. Finally, I managed to put my inhibitions aside and decided to take the "bull by the horns." I called the interviewer back. In the interim, he had apparently checked my references and had concluded that although I did not have prior experience in the microwave field, I could learn.

"But we're moving to Boulder, Colorado, in a few months," he said. "Are you prepared to come with us?"

"Yes, most definitely," I assured him.

With this assurance, he reluctantly agreed to accept me as part of their staff. A few months later, the US government moved us to Colorado.

The skeleton crew who moved to Boulder had many opportunities for advancement. At the NBS, I inherited the task of improving existing methods for measuring microwave power and related quantities—or developing new methods. In a short time, I was able to add some refinements to a measurement technique which the previous staff had initiated and left partially completed.

Since the microwave community had substantial interest in measuring microwave power, I was able to report on my work before an international audience at the 1957 triennial meeting of the International Union of Radio Science held in Boulder, Colorado. I made another presentation to the same organization three years later, this time in London. After another three years, I presented a paper in Tokyo. More trips to Europe and other conferences followed, as numerous technical papers flowed from my pen. The US Patent and Trademark's Office issued patents with my name as the inventor. My reputation in the scientific community grew, and I was invited to present an introductory paper at the International Microwave Conference in Budapest, Hungary.

Prior to my arrival in Budapest, I had been given the name of a Hungarian lady who had worked at a US Army camp during WWII and had acquired a smattering knowledge of English. Following our initial telephone contact, she came to the hotel where I was staying but immediately wanted me to join her and her husband in their car where we could visit without fear of being overheard. I learned a little of how much one's lot in life is fixed when living behind the Iron Curtain. The options for improving one's standard of living by additional education, work, or ambition, apparently did not exist.

Following my presentation, a man from East Germany asked if he could visit with me.

"I have some spare time tomorrow afternoon. Why don't we find a convenient place where we can visit?" I replied.

"Could we go down and walk along the Danube?" he countered.

Although his English vocabulary was quite limited, his pronunciation was surprisingly good. During our conversation he asked me, "Do the people here look different than in the US?"

"Yes," I replied. "I think the people in Budapest would probably be much happier if the occupying army would go home and leave them alone."

He didn't answer, but the look on his face told it all ... "And believe me, they aren't the only ones."

Near the end of our conversation, he said, "I hope that you might be able to come to East Germany if a microwave conference is held there."

"I hope you might be able to visit the United States someday," I replied.

Again, he rewarded me with that piercing look which said, "How could I be so lucky?" As we parted, I had the distinct feeling that, for him, I had been a touch with freedom. The lifestyle I enjoyed was one about which he could only dream.

While waiting for my flight out of Budapest, the Swiss Air crew briefly came into the departure lounge. I looked at their faces. What a contrast between them and the general population I'd been observing for the past three days.

Onboard the aircraft, I found myself seated next to a fellow conference attendee from Italy. Although by US standards my living style would probably be considered no more than modest, by his standards I would probably be "filthy rich." He had apparently been making the same observations I had been making, and as we watched the pilot rev the engines for a short field takeoff, he offered an interesting comment to the effect that "it's not so much where one is in life, but the direction in which one is going."

In time, these experiences helped revive my dormant interest in obtaining an advanced degree. I discovered, to my delight, that my combination of postgraduate classes taken at the Universities of Michigan, Maryland, and Colorado nearly qualified me for a doctorate. I just needed language courses, a few additional classes, and a doctoral thesis which my current research at the NBS would satisfy. With a minimum amount of additional work, I received my PhD in electrical engineering. I'd come a long way from that ten-year-old boy who built a crystal set radio.

I opened the glass door of the NBS building and walked down the hall, as I'd done hundreds of times in the past two decades. Nearby, the atomic cesium clock kept the nation's time—accurate to one second every hundred million years or so. Entering the metrology section, I went into my office, hung up my coat, set my lunch down, and stepped across the hall to the metrology lab that I shared with several others. Cletus looked up.

"Good morning, Clete," I said. We started chatting about the new instruments we were developing to measure microwaves.

Suddenly the door opened. We looked up in surprise as our division chief entered unannounced.

"Hello, Chief," we greeted him.

"Say fellows," he addressed the two of us, "I see there is a metrology conference in Brighton this fall. I suggest that one of you go over there, give them an update on what we are doing here, and bring back a report of what else is going on." Having delivered his message, the division chief disappeared.

I looked at Cletus, and he looked at me.

Cletus and I had developed a measurement technique known as the "six-port."[3] The division chief wanted us to report on this work in Brighton, England.

"Papers" or reports at scientific meetings help people avoid duplicating the work of others with similar objectives. Scientists describe their own work, listen to the reports of others, and engage in dialogue on the best methods to deal with problems of mutual interest. Moreover, because NBS was interested in the work of other national laboratories doing similar work, the scientific meetings we attended were often international.

Although I had already attended and presented papers at a number of meetings, this assignment was unique for a number of reasons. Usually, the author of a paper initiates arrangements to present at scientific meetings. The division chief usually judges a proposed paper to see if it would reflect to the credit of the NBS and whether it would have enough technical merit to justify travel expenses. This time the division chief had suggested the paper.

From my perspective, this chance was a real prize. Brighton is a resort town on the English Channel, approximately 150 miles south of London. As an extra bonus, government travel regulations permit spending extra time at the destination, providing the scientist pays for the extra expense and uses vacation time for the extra days. Over the years, this provision had become a "fringe benefit." Since the government paid my fare, I had been able to take my wife Sadie along on many trips abroad.

"Well, Clete," I said reluctantly, finally breaking the silence, "I got to go last time. I guess it's your turn." I paused. "Of course," I quickly added, "if for any reason you don't want to, I'll be glad to go."

---

3   The name is not expected to be meaningful to the average reader. However, because of the role it plays in the story to follow, it is necessary to give it some sort of name, and it might as well be the technical one. Ultimately, Cletus and I received the Department of Commerce gold medal for this work.

A few days later Cletus found me. "Because of other commitments, I'm not particularly interested in making that trip. If you want to accept the responsibility, it's fine with me."

I was delighted but also surprised; it was unusual for Cletus to have little interest in this opportunity. Scientists have good incentive to present papers. Participating in meetings usually enhances one's stature in the scientific community, and supervisors consider papers presented during a person's annual performance review.

With the assignment now my responsibility, I got busy. First, I needed to submit an abstract or brief description of my proposed contribution to the organizing committee in Brighton. Since I would be going across the Atlantic, I also wanted to find other opportunities while I was there. I discovered the European Microwave Conference would be held in Copenhagen that year.

> **"**
>
> **For some weeks I anxiously awaited a response, hoping I could also go to Denmark. At that point, I had no idea that God would use me to help heal the wounds of my relatives still in Denmark. I knew my family's history but had not yet realized the depth of the pain.**
>
> **"**

Perhaps I could include it as well, I mused. *In doing so, I might also be able to visit my relatives in Denmark, the place of my father's birth.* Then I looked at the dates. To my consternation, I noted that the European Microwave Conference was scheduled for the same time as the Brighton meeting. I kept thinking. *No doubt there are others who would like to attend both conferences. Perhaps the organizers of the Brighton meeting are unaware of the time conflict.*

Since there had been a prior precedent for date-changing, I wondered if the organizers would change the date this time. Anyway, because the deadline for submissions to the European Microwave Conference was close at hand, I decided to submit an abstract to them as well. I also wrote the organizers of the Brighton meeting to ask if there might be change of date in the offing.

For some weeks I anxiously awaited a response, hoping I could also go to Denmark. At that point, I had no idea that God would use me to help heal the wounds of my relatives still in Denmark. I knew my family's history but had not yet realized the depth of the pain.

Chapter 3

My Grandfather Engen[4] had two marriages. My father was one of four children with Grandfather's first wife. Dad's mother died of tuberculosis when he was approximately eight years old. Grandfather Engen remarried some years later, and with his second wife he had six more children.

Dad had an older sister, and when Grandfather remarried, she was well into her teens. It is not possible to reconstruct, from the currently available information, either a detailed or objective account of what happened next. Nor would there be any merit in recounting the sorry tale if it were possible. Suffice it to say that an intense conflict developed between the older sister and the new stepmother. In the years following her mother's death, the older sister had probably become a mother figure to her younger siblings and resented the intrusion of a new member into the family. On the other hand, the stepmother no doubt had a burden to bring some sort of order into what was probably a disorganized household. And what of the younger siblings who were exposed to the conflict? Where did their loyalties lie?

Ultimately, the older sister joined the then-ongoing mass migration of Danish citizens to America. Dad soon followed after completing military service in Denmark. The remaining two siblings from Grandfather's first marriage followed a few years later. Grandfather Engen never again saw his children from his first marriage. The pain felt by the stepmother, as well as Grandfather, can only be imagined.

As a child, I recall frequently getting letters from Denmark with unique stamps which we children loved to collect. However, the letters came to an abrupt end when my father received word of Grandfather's death.

In Dad's later years, and after having raised a family of his own, Dad would probably have admitted or recognized that his stepmother had been "good" for the family, or at least for his father. However, those were probably not the feelings of a young man barely out of his teens. Be that as it may, I believe that Dad never had any conception of the magnitude and depth of the scars which they had left behind in Denmark.

Years later I saw the depth of the pain in retrospect when Dad's half sister, Aunt Emma, commented, "Oh that Mother could have lived to see this day. To

---

4   The actual family name was Christensen. The older children adopted the name Engen after the farm they had come from.

think that the time would come when I would be entertaining Oscar's [Dad's] children in my home!"

However, during this time of preparing for a conference, I merely thought it would be nice to see the relatives whom I had met once before some years earlier when attending another conference.

Chapter 4

I n time I received a reply from the conference organizers. They were aware of the time conflict but, unfortunately, the date was fixed. Because, obviously, I could not be in two places at once, I wrote the European Microwave Conference in Denmark, explaining. "I won't be able to attend. Thus, I am withdrawing the paper that I submitted."

Then I started to make travel arrangements. However, when I checked on airline schedules and ticket prices, to my dismay, I discovered that the fares had increased substantially. Although the NBS covered my fare, I had planned to take my wife Sadie with me since she loved to travel. At the time, the family budget was a bit tight. I started questioning, *Do I (we) really want to make this trip? After all, we've been to Europe a number of times and crossing the Atlantic has lost most of its novelty. Perhaps the anticipated expenses could be better used elsewhere.*

With my misgivings, I approached the division chief.

"You know," I began the conversation, "I've been thinking about this meeting in Brighton and wondering if it might be a useful idea to let Ernie go and present the paper." Then I quickly added, "It's true that he isn't as familiar with the technical details, has less experience, and might not put on as good a show … but then there was a time when I had to get started too. The attention this work has received is, to a large measure, due to his behind-the-scenes effort."

"NO!" the division chief responded quickly and to the point.

I went back to the drawing board and called airlines and travel agencies and consulted travel brochures. Finally, I found a possibility. A local travel agency offered charter flights between Denver and London at a substantially reduced fare. Although these flights required a three-week stay in England, the timing of one of them overlapped the Brighton meeting.

"Perhaps this is the solution," I told Sadie. "We can spend a few days prior to the meeting recovering from jet lag. Following the meeting, we can visit Scotland."

"Oh, Glenn," Sadie replied excitedly. "That sounds like fun."

"Well, there might be one potential problem. Ordinarily, the NBS travel office makes all arrangements for official NBS government business travel. Regulations prevent them from dealing with a commercially operated travel agency. But I'll ask them."

I showed the people in the NBS travel office the information. "Would it be possible for me to purchase a fare on this charter flight instead of you making arrangements?"

The travel arranger looked it over carefully. "Why, yes. I think it would be possible. Under the circumstances and since there will be a reduced cost to the government and NBS, you may purchase both tickets and get reimbursement for your portion."

I smiled at this response but had another question. "What happens to my fare if I break a leg or for some other unforeseen and compelling reason I can't go?"

"As long as this trip has official approval, the NBS will refund you for your portion of the ticket—even though the travel agency cannot give refunds for charter flights."

This seemed too good to be true. "Thank you very much," I said as I hurried out the door to buy the tickets.

"It's all working out," I told Sadie. "We're going on the charter flight."

Sadie called her friend Miriam and told her about our trip.

"Oh, that sounds so exciting," Miriam said. "I would love to go to England and Scotland. I wonder if I could get a ticket also." But to her dismay, she learned that the trip was fully booked.

A few days later I received the official program from the European Microwave Conference in Denmark. Surprisingly, I found my name still listed as a presenter, in spite of my earlier letter withdrawing my submission. Soon I also received the schedule for the Brighton meeting. Upon comparing the two, I learned that I was scheduled to speak in Copenhagen on a Monday afternoon, and in Brighton the following Wednesday. Perhaps I could make both presentations after all.

I looked at the airline guide. Yes, it would be possible. I could fly from London to Copenhagen on Sunday, present my paper on Monday and take the evening flight back to London. After spending the night there, I could take the morning train to Brighton, arriving Tuesday afternoon, in plenty of time for the Wednesday meeting. I presented this change in plans to the Division Chief. As I anticipated, he approved it. Then I wrote to the European Microwave Conference telling them that I would be able to come after all. At that moment I wasn't thinking of my relatives but only about how to meet my commitments and present my paper.

It looked like everything was going to work out. That's only what it looked like.

Chapter 5

By Friday evening before our Wednesday flight from Denver to London, Sadie had completed her shopping. We had thoroughly cleaned the house. We had notified our families of our travel plans. We had packed our suitcases except for a few last-minute items. After the usual hustle and bustle before a major trip, we prepared to spend a relaxing and uneventful Friday evening.

A telephone call interrupted the evening.

I answered. "Hello."

"Hello, Glenn."

I recognized the voice of my brother Hartman who lived in a suburb of Washington, D.C.

"Dad has had a heart attack and is in the Washington Sanitarium and Hospital."

"Oh." I felt stunned. "That is to say, how is he now?"

"His condition has stabilized. You know, he has survived prior heart attacks."

"Perhaps this one is not too serious."

The rest of the evening Sadie and I reviewed God's promises and lifted Dad up to God in prayer. Having done this, we retired for the night. But when the telephone rang again at 3:00 a.m. the following morning, we knew before answering it that Dad had gone to his rest.

Needless to say, our priorities immediately changed. We needed to get to Washington, D.C. for the funeral. As soon as possible we booked an early afternoon flight. But what were we going to do about my commitment to the conferences in Europe? What about those nonrefundable airplane tickets I had purchased to London? Obviously, we wouldn't be able to go to Washington, D.C. for the funeral and return to Denver in time for the Wednesday charter flight to London. But were there other options?

Perhaps I could continue on from Washington, but given the emotional trauma I was experiencing, would I be up to it? Perhaps Cletus could go, or given the change in circumstances, the division chief might be willing to let Ernie do it after all. In that case, perhaps he could use our tickets. First, however, we would have to find out if Ernie would be interested.

As soon as it was prudent, we called. Because of other commitments, Cletus couldn't go. Ernie was interested, provided his wife could go too, but she didn't have a passport. He would see if she could get one on short notice.

For the remainder of the morning, we repacked our suitcases for a funeral. I gathered up the few things I might need in case I ended up going on to Europe. Of one thing I was certain. If I did go to London, I would be going alone and would return as soon as possible. Although Sadie was disappointed, the idea of a two-week vacation in Scotland had completely lost its appeal.

As we flew to Washington that afternoon, one thought continually dominated my thinking. *Of all times, and given all the hassle in arranging our trip to Europe, why did this have to happen now? Why indeed?* A week earlier, a month later, my current dilemma could have been avoided. Why did my mind have to be burdened with the problem of what to do with those charter tickets we couldn't possibly use, when I would much rather be dealing with the loss of my father who had been such a blessing to me?

Why God? Why?? And where are my priorities? Am I really more concerned with my impending financial loss than with the death of my father?

Given the circumstances, and the prior commitment from the NBS travel office, I was reasonably sure that, at most, I would only lose the cost of one of the tickets, but this provided little comfort.

My brother Hartman met us in Washington, D.C. "I've been in touch with Josephine Cunnington Edwards," he said. "She's agreed to fly up from Tennessee and have the funeral service. It's been scheduled for Monday afternoon."

Josephine Cunnington Edwards had authored the book, *Son of the Vikings*, which detailed my father's experience in the Danish Army. He had faced court-martial and a life sentence in prison for staying true to his convictions and then had been miraculously pardoned.

My sister, Ruth, and her husband, Bob, arrived from California the next day, Sunday. I couldn't do anything about the tickets until Monday morning. At first, I wanted to call the charter airline but then decided that someone in Boulder could handle the problem better by working directly with the travel agency. I called Ernie, explained the problem, and he went to work.

About a half hour before we left for the funeral, Ernie called back. First, although his wife could get a passport in Chicago on a walk-in basis, this would involve more hassle than they wanted to accept. Thus, Ernie would not be making the trip.

Second, the travel agency absolutely refused to give a refund for those tickets.

Third, the division chief came on the line. "Glenn, I was certainly sorry to hear about the death of your father."

"Thank you. It has been a huge loss."

Then he continued. "Also, it seems that there has been some misunderstanding. There is absolutely no way we [NBS] can reimburse you for that ticket you've purchased...."

Chapter 6

I was stuck—not with just one unusable ticket but with two. It wasn't just about the money; it was how I felt about myself. I'd always tried to be prudent and careful in using of money. The impending loss of the price of those tickets due to my misjudgment was almost more than I could handle.

As I made my way to the funeral, again the question burned within my heart, *Why did I have to receive this news just now? It would have been soon enough to get that message after the funeral.* In retrospect, the words of a beautiful song describe my experience well.

O what peace we often forfeit,
O what needless pain we bear,
All because we do not carry
Everything to God in prayer.[5]

And so, with thoughts of financial disaster competing for my attention, I went to the funeral. I knew Mrs. Edwards would have something well worth hearing. What could I do to clear my mind of these problems so that I could concentrate on her message? The cold, hard pew pressed into my back as somber people filed into the church. After a few more or less typical preliminaries, Mrs. Edwards stood up to speak.

I believe one of the most sorrowful and terrible funerals that ever was held, was held near a garden eastward in Eden. There were no kind people to aid the hands of Adam and Eve when they scooped out a grave for their sweet son Abel. There was no music, no minister. And it was Adam and Eve who prepared the body of their dear son. Their anguish was a torture because of their realization that it was because of their own sins that this terrible thing had happened. And then they had one little gleam of a promise that God had given them when He promised that this enemy should one day be put underfoot.

And this was a foreshadowing of another, an even more terrible funeral, 4,000 years later, when at the 'place of the skull' the 'second Adam' laid down His life as a criminal. He was pierced with the iron nails that He had made, iron that He had made on the day of Creation. The wood for the rough cross on which He was slain grew by the power of our Creator, Jesus Christ. Those whom He loved, and whom He came to save, vented their shame, their rage, and their hate upon His dear, sweet sacrifice.

---

5   John M. Scriven, "What a Friend We Have in Jesus," The Seventh-day Adventist Hymnal (Hagerstown, MD: Review and Herald Publishing Association, 1985).

But that was the foreshadowing of another funeral which has not been yet, which I look forward to with great anticipation. And it shan't be long from now because it will be the funeral of death itself. I'll be so glad when Jesus, our Savior ... and the angels will sing, and the heavenly hosts will shout for joy, and death and sorrow and sighing will be no more. For countless centuries, vengeful death has galloped down the corridors of time on his evil black horse, making tears of sorrow and wailing and anguish in a world that is rent with sorrow. But I praise Almighty God that this funeral is soon to take place, when death will be no more. When Jesus comes, the bands of death will be broken forever.

I want to give tribute today to the ending of a beautiful, a lovely life. I'm so glad that my life has touched the Engens' lives. I'm so glad for the letter I got one day, from Glenn, giving me a little bit of the story of a man....

And after I got this letter, I wanted to meet this man.... And I had that beautiful privilege. Day after day, there in Battle Creek ... I think that only in the annals of the book of life will we ever find out all the influence that he had, even in the little country of Denmark, when for the first time in the history of that country, a young man stood up and was willing to be counted, was willing to endure prison for life, rather than to sacrifice a principle.

One of these days when Jesus comes, there'll be a little grave opened in northern Denmark, and Oscar Engen's mother will come forth.... I remember one thing that he [Oscar] told me again and again. He said, 'I am the man that I am today because of my faithful mother.' And when I think he only had that mother about eight years, what a woman she must have been.... For over 100 years now that lovely life is still glowing....

I got to go to that prison where Oscar was incarcerated.... And when I think of this wonderful young man who with just six months at Skodsborg [the place where he became an Adventist], awakened again to fulfill the prayers of a righteous mother, which made him so firm and so staunch that he was willing to yield up his life, his freedom, rather than sacrifice truth, it makes me wonder how many people there are in the world with such a staunch and wonderful background. He told me that one day, while he was sitting in the prison this day ... he heard the shriek of the train and knew [his sister] Anna was in the station waiting for him, and he had said, 'If I'm not there you'll know I'm in trouble.' He was in trouble, in bad trouble, in terrible trouble. And then there were whispers which came to him, 'Why not give it up and wait two years, come back to it in two years?' The temptation was almost too much. He told me, 'I never went through such anguish and such misery in my life. I thought there'd be other young men, like my younger brother and other people that maybe had been converted at Skodsborg, that will have a terrible time because I've given up … and … I'll not do it. I'll not do it. I'll not give it up.' So, when they came to him, and asked him before that dreadful, unfair, terrible court-martial, 'Well, are you going to fall in line?'

'No, I can't. I must live the life. I must do what's right.'

And then that travesty of a court-martial—when he was accused of things that he didn't do at all.… But I'm happy for one thing. The devil often overdoes. He goes a little too far. How his enemies must have gloated when the sentence was so terribly drastic: prison for life, for a young boy in his early twenties, a lot of that time to be spent in a dungeon without enough light even to see to read by, on bread and water for weeks at a time. It takes a staunch soul to resist that.

But the devil overdid himself. What Oscar and a lot of these others didn't know was that for such a terrible, horrible sentence, it had to have the signature of the head of the whole Danish military. And so, this sentence was sent to Copenhagen, and it was so terrible that the head of the military searched the records to see what this young man could possibly have done to have merited such a terrible, terrible sentence. And he couldn't find it. All the time this young man was waiting, not knowing that angels were flying to and fro in his behalf, not knowing that on the other side of the world lay a work for him to do that hardly anybody else could do. The Lord had his work laid out for him.

And then, when he was summoned to Copenhagen, he had no idea but that he might be stood up and shot right there. The clouds of World War I were getting thicker. Everybody knew about the hotbed down in the Balkans. Everybody in all Europe had known about the Berlin to Baghdad railroad and the ambitions of the Kaiser. It hadn't been many years since a part of Denmark [Schleswig-Holstein] had been seized by Germany. So, all Europe was nervous. And this young man went on that long journey, down the peninsula, and over toward Copenhagen, not knowing that he'd ever come back. Only to find, to his joy, and his delight, that he had been pardoned by the king of Denmark.

I think that it is a wonderful thing that we can draw an analogy from this. Down through the long ages, the accuser of the brethren has been on our backs, like rakes across our tender flesh. He's accused us of everything. He has wrung our hearts with sorrow; he has torn from us our dearest treasures. One of these days—how precious it will be—we're going to take a journey, a wonderful journey, and we'll meet our loved ones in the air. Won't that be beautiful? 'Behold, I shew you a mystery; We shall not all sleep, but we shall all be changed, in a moment, in the twinkling of an eye, at the last trump: for the trumpet shall sound, and the dead shall be raised incorruptible.'[6] And then shall be brought to pass the saying that is written: 'Death is swallowed up in victory. O death, where is thy sting? O grave, where is thy victory?'[7] We'll be on our way to meet the King. Won't it be a wonderful thing? We're going to the very seat of the kingdom, as Oscar did. And we'll receive the pardon from our King. And there'll be no graves on the hillside.

Oscar, as a healer with his wife, has given comfort to many a sufferer. He was surrounded by love and tender kindness when he passed away. And when he opens his eyes again, he'll behold the face of our beautiful Savior. I thank God for that.

Dear Brother Engen, the long, hard road has passed. The Lord has bid thee, 'Lay thy burden down.' A rest so long deserved is yours at last. Yea, soon you will have a victor's crown. The Lord hath allowed thee rest before the storm, before the time of trouble breaks on man. You'll sweetly sleep; you'll never feel all that anguish. And soon our Lord will give you life again. How sweet when next your eyes behold the light; it will be the glow of victory and grace. How sweet to know when you shall next awake you will behold our Savior's loving face.

And so, I would give a tribute to a great man, a modern Huss, a modern Jerome, a modern Wycliff. A man who was willing to die rather than sacrifice a principle. I know that as surely as I get to the kingdom of our

---

6   1 Corinthians 15:51–52.
7   1 Corinthians 15:54–55.

Father, I'll meet Oscar Engen there, and he'll have many that he has led to the truth.[8]

As I sat there listening, I realized that Mrs. Edwards' words included the idea that Dad's life and experience still had a message for the people of Denmark. In that moment, I had an experience which I can only describe as the Lord giving me a burning realization and conviction: I had a place in this story. I would have a role to play in carrying this message to the other parts of my family in Denmark.

As I thought about my family in Denmark, my conviction grew that if there was ever a time that they might be receptive to hearing more about the unique beliefs which had motivated Dad's life, this was the time. Right now, those events were being recorded on tape. But before sharing the tape, first, maybe … just maybe … some fences might need mending.

> **As I thought about my family in Denmark, my conviction grew that if there was ever a time that they might be receptive to hearing more about the unique beliefs which had motivated Dad's life, this was the time.**

In any case I became convinced that I needed to fly to Denmark and then, on Dad's behalf (not my own), and in company with Aunt Emma, whom we had visited on a number of previous occasions, I needed to put flowers on the graves of his father, his stepmother, and then on that of his own mother (who was buried in a different cemetery).

---

8   Josephine Cunnington Edwards. Funeral service for Oscar Engen, Excerpts from the cassette recording, August 29, 1977. More of the details of Dad's experience in the Danish army are found in Mrs. Edwards book *Son of the Vikings* (available from TEACH Services). Dad's mother and her brother, Carl Ottosen, were among some of the earliest converts to Adventism in Denmark. Dad had accepted the Adventist message during a six-month visit to his uncle (Carl Ottosen) who had founded Skodsborg Sanitarium, just prior to his being inducted into the Danish army. When Dad refused to participate in the military training exercises on Saturday, there was little sympathy for his religious objections.

It was Dad's understanding, and upon which the book was based, that the court-martial had sentenced him to life imprisonment, with the further stipulation that in the event of war, he was to be shot…. But Dad most certainly would never have approved the analogy between himself and Huss, Jerome, or Wycliff. His military service was completed in Copenhagen, where his religious beliefs were respected. Shortly after completing his military service, Dad immigrated to the United States where he met my mother while in nurse's training at the New England Sanitarium.

In the interests of accuracy, and as the author learned as the story unfolds, some of the details, as recounted by Mrs. Edwards, were probably incorrect. Others were somewhat embellished by her, no doubt for the benefit of the family, who constituted the majority of those at the funeral.

As the idea took shape, I also realized that the timing was perfect. *Absolutely perfect!!* I thought. I could spend a few more days with my family in Washington. Next, I would fly over to Copenhagen, then up to Aalborg (where Dad's court-martial had been held), rent a car, drive the remaining thirty miles or so to Hjorring, where Aunt Emma lived, and spend the weekend with her. Then, on Sunday afternoon, I could return to Copenhagen, present my paper the following day, and continue my trip as originally planned.

The turmoil I had gone through just an hour earlier had been completely swept out the door and had evaporated like the morning dew. Peace and joy, such as I had never before known or felt, flooded my heart. From my personal experience I can attest that, nothing can make you sad, when Jesus makes you glad![9] The $900 worth of (useless!) airplane tickets no longer mattered. Somehow, I'd gotten my head put back on straight. I'd gotten my priorities straightened out. Everything was going to be all right!

---

9   Ellen G. White, "The Peace that Passeth All Understanding," The Signs of the Times, December 27, 1905.

Chapter 7

Back at the house after the funeral, the telephone rang. It was my division chief. "Glenn, I was mistaken when I told you we couldn't pay for your ticket. It's true that I can't make that decision. It will have to be made in Washington, but under the circumstances, we really don't expect you to go."

"It's not really that important anymore," I replied. "I've thought it over and decided that I'm going. It doesn't matter if I get reimbursed for the ticket or not."

After a long pause, the division chief replied, "Well, it's certainly up to you, but I should probably tell you that if you do end up going, that could very well prejudice the decision against you about getting any reimbursement."

Once again, I replied, "That doesn't matter."

It was now late Monday afternoon. However, I had a couple of ideas I wanted to try for the tickets. Although the rules governing charter flights were strict, if we could find someone else who wanted to go, they might be able to use the tickets.

Our friend, Miriam, back in Boulder, loved to travel. She had tried to get a reservation on the same charter flight, only to be told that the plane was fully booked. Sadie called her.

"Miriam, would you like to use one of our tickets on the charter flight?"

"Yes, of course, I'd love to go. But I don't want to travel alone. I need a traveling companion."

"I have an aunt in Phoenix," Sadie told her. "I'll call her."

Sadie dialed Aunt Martha's number.

"Hello, Aunt Martha." Sadie explained the situation. "Would you like to go to England with my friend Miriam?"

"Yes, I'd like to go, but I don't have a passport."

"We found out from Glenn's colleague that it's possible to get a passport in Chicago in one day by going to the passport office in person. Maybe you could get one in Los Angeles."

"Los Angeles isn't exactly on the route between Phoenix and Denver! But anyway, I have a hair appointment tomorrow morning at nine o'clock. I'll move it up to eight o'clock just in case."

The next morning, Tuesday, Aunt Martha called the passport office.

"Yes, we can get you a passport if you come to our office in Los Angeles," the receptionist told her.

It was now nine o'clock. A flight would go to Los Angeles at eleven o'clock. Aunt Martha had exactly two hours to pack a suitcase for a three-week trip to England—and catch the flight, but she made it, with ten minutes to spare.

After a long taxi ride, Aunt Martha walked into the passport office early Tuesday afternoon. She stepped up to the counter and said, "I need to get a passport."

The clerk took a hard look at her and finally replied, "Well, lady, this is really very irregular." With that, the clerk prepared to send her out the door.

"Excuse me, lady," someone spoke behind her.

Aunt Martha turned.

"Did I understand that you want a passport? Just come this way, please."

By 4 p.m. she had a passport! She grabbed a taxi for the airport and caught the 5:30 p.m. plane for Denver where Miriam met her. The next morning, they were on their way to London.

* * * * *

While Aunt Martha had been getting her passport, I called the travel agency in Boulder and made arrangements to change the tickets. "It's all settled," I commented to my sister-in-law Clara as I put down the phone. "It looks like we've gotten rid of those tickets."

"And now Sadie can go too, can't she?"

I looked at her, surprised. Up to that point the idea hadn't even crossed my mind. Before we left Boulder for Dad's funeral, I had concluded that, if I went at all, I would be going alone. Yet, when I picked up my passport, on an impulse which I couldn't have explained at the time, I had picked up Sadie's passport as well.

Although the inspiration I had gained from Mrs. Edwards message had also brought new strength and vigor, the trip would nevertheless be tiring and demanding. What better source of additional strength and encouragement could I have than that provided by my dear companion?

I found Sadie. "Could we have a family consultation?" I asked. I knew before asking about Europe what her response would be—even though her funeral wardrobe was hardly adequate for a three-week trip to Europe. "You can go shopping," I told her.

She hurried out to buy some appropriate clothes. I felt pretty good, being off the hook for about $900 worth of Denver to London tickets. I called the travel agency in Washington, D.C. which had worked out my revised itinerary to Europe and told them to write up a second set of tickets.

We took an interlude for a couple of days, squeezing into my brother's motorhome and traveling to New England where we visited other relatives. Then, on Thursday, Sadie and I flew for Denmark. I had the most unlikely collection of items with me, but the tape recording of the funeral service was of primary importance, along with a battery-operated tape recorder I had borrowed.

"God, if You want to make the words on this tape come out in Danish, I know that will be a small thing for You," I prayed. With that, I put the matter from my mind and fell asleep somewhere over the Atlantic Ocean.

> **"**
>
> *"God, if You want to make the words on this tape come out in Danish, I know that will be a small thing for You," I prayed. With that, I put the matter from my mind and fell asleep somewhere over the Atlantic Ocean.*
>
> **"**

Chapter 8

Right on schedule on Friday evening, we arrived by rental car at Aunt Emma's home in Hjorring, Denmark. Aunt Emma's daughter, Agnete, who lived in Aalborg, had arrived only a few hours earlier, after making the same trip we had made. In contrast to her mother, Agnete had a good command of English. After our initial greeting, Aunt Emma said, "With Oscar gone, I was afraid you wouldn't come to visit me anymore. I would never see you again."

"Oh no, that's not true. If anything, the opposite is true. With Dad gone, you now have a double role—not only Aunt Emma but also as a substitute for Dad."

Although I had dismissed her thoughts initially, later I reflected and concluded that, although completely unfounded, her fears may have been real. I remembered how letters between Denmark and America had stopped when her father, Grandpa Engen, had passed away. Grandpa Engen's first family had still not reconciled themselves to their stepmother.

As I sized up the situation at Aunt Emma's house, I realized that Agnete planned to take us back to Aalborg with her. I called her aside.

"Look," I said, "I probably should have been in touch with you earlier. I could have come by your house and saved you the trip up here. But it looks as if this sofa in the living room also makes into a bed. Perhaps we can stay here for the night."

Then I explained my plan of putting flowers on the graves, and concluded, "Perhaps in this way, we could give your mother a message which might be difficult to put into words."

"Glenn, I agree," Agnete responded quickly. Then, pausing for effect, she softly added, "I think you already have!"

The next morning, after a breakfast which only Aunt Emma could have prepared, we made our way to the little church in Elling. This church was located a scant quarter of a mile from the Engen farm, the farm from which the children by Grandfather's first marriage had taken their family name after arriving in America. The church was rich in family history. In keeping with family tradition, here Dad had been confirmed into the Lutheran faith years before he had become a Seventh-day Adventist. In the cemetery adjoining the church, Dad's father, his stepmother, and other family members had been laid to rest in the family burial plot.

We found the graves of Dad's father and step-mother and laid flowers on each of them. After laying the flowers, we drove a few miles south to Frederickshavn, to the cemetery where Dad's mother had been buried. However, we were unable to locate her grave.[10]

Since time was pressing, we then made our way to the home of Anna, one of Dad's cousins on his mother's side, who was expecting us for the noon meal. Anna also belonged to the Adventist faith.

Mealtime in Denmark is usually a special occasion, and this meal was no exception. With the meal completed and the dishes put away, it was time to bring out the recorder and share, if possible, the message on the tape. The four of us assembled in the living room. The tape began with musical selections, and these presented no problem. However, I especially wanted them to hear Mrs. Edwards' comments.

When we reached her words, I immediately realized that we were in trouble. We were in big trouble! Anna's understanding of English was even more limited than that of Aunt Emma. I knew nothing of Danish. I had stopped the recorder after Mrs. Edwards' first sentence or two, and asked if they understood, only to see them shaking their heads, "No."

I had then backed the recorder up and tried again. Same response. Another try; same response. Although my belief in God's ability to make some internal modifications to the tape recorder was unshaken, apparently it wasn't going to happen. The words emerging from the loudspeaker were still in English. *So! Where do we go from here?* Had God overlooked this problem?

---

10   In the absence of a given level of interest by the surviving family, it is the practice in Denmark to "reuse" the burial site after a certain number of years have elapsed. Although we had been to the grave a number of years earlier, it is quite possible that the site had been reallocated in the interim.

Chapter 9

At that very moment someone knocked at the door. We looked up startled. Who could that be? Upon opening the door, we found the local Adventist pastor. He had attended Newbold College in England. Thus, he knew English and, of course, he knew Danish. We returned to the tape recording. This time I let Mrs. Edwards speak a few sentences and then paused while our guest translated them into Danish.

When Mrs. Edwards had finished, I saw that the pastor also had been obviously moved by her message. "By the way," I said to him, "would you like to have a copy of that tape?"

"Brother, would I!" he exclaimed. "There's material there for at least a half dozen sermons. Of course, I'll pay for it," he quickly added.

"That won't be necessary," I assured him. "I'll have a copy made as soon as I return home, and you can forget about any payment!"

How did it happen that the pastor had come to visit at that particular time? In the conversation that followed, he told us that during that very week, he had been reading Edwards' book, *Son of the Vikings*, the story of my father. Earlier that very Sabbath he had commented on the book to Anna and concluded, "I would certainly like to meet that man someday!"

"Well," Anna replied, "I'm expecting his son to be in my home this afternoon. Would you like to come over?"

He did. And then his timing. God's timing? Had the pastor arrived fifteen minutes earlier, courtesy would have dictated that we visit with him. I doubt that I would have thought of using him as a translator. Had he arrived five minutes later, I probably would have already put away the tape recorder and abandoned the idea of sharing Mrs. Edwards' message as an exercise in futility. No, at the exact moment he was needed, he was there. Do such things happen by mere accident?

Finally, there was the matter of the atmosphere in which this message was shared. Because of our limited ability to converse in each other's language, we had never talked about religion with Aunt Emma. Although as a Lutheran, she certainly believed in the hereafter and the promise of being one day reunited with loved ones, she may have not been entirely comfortable with other elements in Mrs. Edwards' tribute.

There is sometimes a thin line between affirming mutually held beliefs and being perceived as doing a "hard sell" in favor of one's own religious affiliation. With her limited familiarity with English, and my nonexistent knowledge of Danish, it would have been all too easy to have crossed that line. As it was, Anna's interest in the message was reason enough to have it translated. Aunt Emma had not been put in the potentially embarrassing position of nodding assent to ideas with which she may not have been entirely comfortable. Although I doubt that she felt uneasy, she had total liberty to ignore the associated conversation should she so choose. Had I been asked to devise a setting in which Mrs. Edwards' message could be shared, I would most certainly have fallen far short of the one which the Lord had arranged.

With his task completed, the pastor bid us farewell, and we soon left for the home of Aunt Emma's son, Peter. Here we reunited with Agnete and her husband, Arne. By early evening we had completed our visit with Peter, bid farewell to Aunt Emma, and made our way back to Aalborg as Agnete had originally planned. After spending the night there, the morning hours passed all too quickly before our flight back to Copenhagen.

Because of the pace with which the past week had unfolded, I'd had little or no time to think of my speaking engagement the following afternoon. Seated in the plane, I dug through my briefcase, found the program schedule, and started refreshing my memory. My activity soon attracted the attention of the gentleman in the airplane seat next to me.

"Excuse me, Sir," he said. "Are you attending the microwave conference?"

"Indeed, I am," I replied.

"Then let me introduce myself," he continued. "My name is Jorgen Andersen. I am affiliated with Aalborg University and was a member of the organizing committee for the conference."

I quickly forgot my interest in the program. We spent the remainder of the trip getting acquainted and discussing technical subjects of mutual interest. I also told him of my family in Denmark and that this was the place of my father's birth. "Someday, I hope I will have the opportunity of returning to Denmark and looking up my family roots," I concluded. By this time, we had reached Copenhagen and we parted. I had no idea how God would use this conversation in the future or the impact that this brief meeting would have.

After presenting my paper the following day, Sadie and I flew back to London where we spent the evening with Miriam and Aunt Martha. Then we traveled on to Brighton and the conference there. Upon its completion, we reunited with Miriam and Aunt Martha and spent the next two weeks touring northern England and Scotland.

When I returned home, I immediately had a duplicate made of the tape which I had promised to the Adventist pastor. Some weeks later I received a letter from the pastor with some exciting news. Josephine Cunnington Edwards' book *Son of the Vikings* was being translated into Danish and her funeral sermon would be added as an appendix.

Thus ended the eventful trip to Europe. For all I knew, that was the end of the story. Or was it?

Chapter 10

Two years passed. Another Friday afternoon as I looked through my mail at work, a Danish stamp caught my attention. Although I commonly received mail from my European colleagues, anything from Denmark held more than average interest. I noted that the return address was Aalborg. I felt excitement building. Quickly tearing the letter open, I read the following lines:

Dear Dr. Engen:

Through Jorgen Bach Anderson [the gentleman whom I had met on the flight from Aalborg to Copenhagen two years earlier] who is working here at Aalborg University Center, we have heard that you are interested in coming to Denmark and do research here at our Institute. We have applied to our National Technical Research Council for money to do research on six-port reflectometers [the six-port, the reader will recall, is a device for microwave measurements in which I had had an active role].… We have applied for (salary) money for you, too, and are glad if you are interested in staying here a month or two to speed up our research in this field of yours.

The letter was signed by a professor at the Aalborg University Center.

I went home and excitedly shared the news with Sadie.

"Glenn, I'm going to have to tie a massive lead weight to your feet to keep you from floating off on a cloud somewhere," she said.

I quickly came down to earth. "It's one thing to receive such an invitation. But it's quite another to obtain the required leave of absence from NBS in order to accept it."

Indeed, the NBS had rather compelling reasons to deny a leave like this. It had to do with the "balance of trade" problem. Quite obviously, the United States can't compete with the cheap labor available in some of the third world countries. The USA's only competitive edge in the international marketplace is with high technology. So why should a government agency, in this case the NBS, give one of its senior scientists a leave of absence to share technology, developed at taxpayer expense, with a foreign university when the technology might ultimately be used to undersell American industry in the international market? Why indeed? One of my colleagues had received a similar invitation some months earlier and, quite understandably, the NBS had denied permission to accept it.

But, having received the invitation, even though I had little expectation that the NBS would approve it, I referred it to the NBS management for formal action. To my utter amazement, a week or so later I learned that

39

not only had it been approved but also instead of being granted a "leave of absence," I would be sent to Denmark on "official business." In practical terms this meant that my salary from NBS, which was somewhat more than that I would have received from Denmark, would continue. More importantly, the NBS would cover the cost of my travel, and I would also receive a substantial allowance to cover my living expenses in Denmark. The money Aalborg University had offered as salary would go to NBS and be used to cover these expenses.

I quickly wrote a letter back to Aalborg University, indicating that I would be coming on official business and telling them that the money which had been set aside for my salary was, instead, to go to NBS to help cover the cost of my trip.

In time I received a reply from Denmark: their rules and regulations would not permit this. The money had to be paid directly to me.

Unfortunately, but as I knew without asking, the rules at NBS were equally inflexible. A number of letters and then telegrams flew across the Atlantic in an effort to resolve the issue. Finally, in a last-ditch effort to break the deadlock, my correspondent in Denmark suggested that "the arrangements between Aalborg University and me were really no concern of NBS management."

Whew! Little did my correspondent know that he had lit a fuse, the other end of which was buried in a keg of dynamite!

What now? Was the whole trip to "go down the tubes?" Although I had been involved in tricky situations before, never had there been one in which so much was at stake. But then, as I considered my options, appropriate words came to mind so quickly I could hardly wait to get them on paper. I knew the Ultimate Source of those words was certainly not my mind.

After acknowledging my correspondent's suggestion, I noted, "Unfortunately, for better or worse, my management has an entirely different view of the matter." I then explained that as a member of the NBS staff, my role fell into the category of a "public official." As such, I could not receive compensation from any source which might possibly be construed as an effort to influence my "official behavior or conduct." Although this was certainly not our intent, this nevertheless provided the basis for certain rules and regulations to which I must give careful adherence. This was an extremely sensitive issue with NBS management.

While waiting for a reply, I studied the regulations. I found a possible option. I could accept the check provided that I did not actually cash it, but rather endorsed it, "pay to the National Bureau of Standards." Under the prevailing circumstances, however, I had little reason to believe that my host in Denmark would find this acceptable. My five-page telegram to Denmark concluded with an outline of this possibility.

Contrary to my expectation, they soon replied that this would be satisfactory. I then presented this "solution" to NBS management and, after it had been reviewed and initialed by five or more levels of NBS management, they accepted the plan and put the issue to rest.

In the interim, however, another problem developed.

Six months or a year prior, Congress had passed a law of which no one in management had been aware until recently. In an effort to contain the ever-increasing federal budget, Congress had decreed that no agency could spend more on travel than they had in the previous fiscal year. Period. Although Denmark was, to a large extent, paying my way, this money had to be funneled through the NBS travel budget. We were now well into the fiscal year. My management had been operating under a travel ceiling of which they had been unaware. Before they had time to react, however, the problem became much larger.

The year was 1980, a census year, which calls for a substantial amount of travel. If Congress held the Census Bureau to the letter of the law, there would be no census that year. However, the Department of Commerce devised a solution to this problem: The other agencies under its administration would curtail their ordinary travel and thus "bail out" the Census Bureau. The National Bureau of Standards was one of these agencies.

After the dust had settled, the management for my group had to assign priorities to all travel proposed for the remainder of the fiscal year. Among the trips considered, one, at best, had marginal justification. If granted, that trip would consume the remaining allotment for travel. Whose trip was that? Mine. My trip to Denmark would mean no travel for anyone else in my group for the remainder of the fiscal year. *Quite obviously, this isn't going to fly*, I thought.

In the government service it sometimes seems that no matter what you want to do, there's always rule against it. But then if you look hard enough, there is usually a way around the rule! So, someone got busy and started looking.

"Let's see. Engen is planning to go over to Aalborg University, isn't he?"

"Yes, that's correct."

"Well, the travel ceiling doesn't apply if he's there on a 'training assignment.'"

Although my primary role in Aalborg would have been better described as a "teacher," almost certainly there would be occasions to also learn from my colleagues. Perhaps I could go that way.

My immediate management ran this idea by a few people in the NBS in Washington and asked, "Do you think you can buy this?"

"Yes, that's OK," they responded. So, another hurdle had been surmounted. (Or so we thought.)

Chapter 11

Then another little problem—actually not so little—developed. With no particular rhyme or reason, Sadie started getting sick at unusual times. True to form, she had thought, *If I ignore this thing, it'll go away."*

But it didn't go away. One Sunday morning, while we were engaged in a project of mutual interest, Sadie asked to be excused and headed for the bedroom. It had taken me a while to catch on, but when I did, we had a little family discussion. I concluded by saying, "You know we're leaving for Denmark in a few months, and I don't want to be running around over there and looking up doctors. Tomorrow you're going to see Dr. Jerry and find out what the problem is. What's more, if you don't, I'm going to leave you home!" (Not really, but I figured that that would get her attention.)

It did get her attention. It didn't take Dr. Jerry Smith long to determine that she had a tumor in her abdomen. I reacted immediately with nonchalance. "Well, that's probably no big deal. If one has an abdominal tumor, the obvious thing to do is open the abdomen, find the offending piece of protoplasm, cut it out (or off), close the incision and then let nature do the rest!" (With insight and aptitude like that, I should have probably been a surgeon!)

But the medical profession didn't seem to be in any hurry to do anything about it. They had to "study" it first. First, they did an ultrasound, then an IVP, an arteriogram, a liver scan, another x-ray, and on and on and on—for about two weeks. From my perspective, I had just about concluded that this would soon become one of the most studied tumors in the history of medicine.

Then one day, one of the urologists in town, who had been called in as a consultant, asked Sadie to come to his office. After pacing the floor, he finally broke the silence by saying, "Several of us have been studying your x-rays and the results of this last test and have concluded that the tumor is attached to one of your kidneys. It's very likely cancer. We need to take out your kidney. But then, you have two kidneys. You really only need one," he quickly added.

"Well, how soon can you do it?" Sadie immediately replied.

"How soon would you like?"

"Tomorrow if possible! After all, I'm leaving for Denmark in eight weeks!!"

The urologist did a double take. Then he looked down at his schedule. "Yes, we can do it tomorrow."

With this settled, Sadie headed home to pick up the few things she would need for her hospital stay.

She called me. "Glenn, they're going to operate tomorrow. The doctor thinks it might be cancer. He said I might need follow-up chemotherapy. Could you please meet me at the hospital?"

Although my feelings had perhaps not reached the threshold of being thoroughly alarmed, I certainly felt more than a little strange to receive that type of prognosis. After all, had they gone ahead and operated on her, that would have been soon enough to have received this type of news. But Sadie did not seem any more concerned than if she'd been going to the dentist to have a tooth filled.

As part of the hospital routine that evening, the nurse gave Sadie the standard consent form to sign for the removal of one of her kidneys. However, it also said, "possible liver resection."

"What does that mean?" we asked.

"In the opinion of the medical staff, the tumor has probably invaded the liver as well."

> **The next morning, for our devotion, I chose to read the twenty-third Psalm. Little did I realize how appropriate it was or how important it would become.**

If that had been the case, it probably would have been terminal. Quite likely, this explained the rather strange look the urologist had given Sadie when, after giving her the news, she had replied, "Let's get this out as soon as possible; I'm leaving for Denmark in eight weeks." As nearly as we can determine, he was probably thinking, "Lady, you're not going anywhere in eight weeks. You'll be lucky if you don't end up in the cemetery!"

All in all, not exactly an exciting prospect.

The next morning, for our devotion, I chose to read the twenty-third Psalm. Little did I realize how appropriate it was or how important it would become. Pastor Jim Hoehn and his wife Roxie came and had prayer with us. How much we appreciated that. Then Sadie was off to surgery and, in a gesture that meant so much to me, a dear friend, Dottie, took time out of her busy schedule to come and await the results with me. In retrospect, I'm afraid I was not a very good host. I paced the floor, and as my kidneys responded sympathetically to Sadie, I used the restroom every few minutes.

In the operating room a different drama unfolded.

Chapter 12

Although the urologist had been called for his expertise in removing the kidney, Dr. Jerry, a surgeon, initiated the procedure. After making the appropriate incision, the nature of the offending tumor was immediately apparent. It was about the size of a tennis ball! But, instead of being attached to the kidney which had been anticipated, it was on the liver and in the worst possible location on the liver. Everyone has two kidneys and ordinarily can get along with one. But people only have one liver. If my understanding is correct, any attempt to remove something from the liver poses a very real danger of creating uncontrolled bleeding.

I've asked myself many times: What would it have been like to be in Dr. Jerry's shoes there in the operating room? What job stress! In addition to being a patient of his, Sadie was also a personal friend. Staring him in the face was the offending tumor. It needed to be removed, yet if he started to cut, would he be able to deal with the resulting flow of blood? Would he have turned to the attending nurse and said, "Quick! Give me the knife; I want to get busy"? I don't think so.

In Dr. Jerry's own words, "I wanted to make a more thorough examination. And so, I slid my hand behind the liver to assure myself that there were no further problems there. Upon removing my hand from the incision, the tumor was in my palm! I hadn't even touched it with a knife!"

"What happened? Did it break off or something?"

"Well, blood vessel tumors of that nature do not 'break off.'"

Although we will have to wait until that "better land" for confirmation, I believe that Sadie's guardian angel, who of course was present, intervened with the unspoken words, "Dr. Jerry, let me give you an assist with this one!"

At this point, with the offending tumor out of the way, there wasn't much left for the medical team to do but close the incision. Sadie soon returned to intensive care. For a few days, her recovery was uneventful.

But then she became increasingly uncomfortable. The doctor tapped her abdomen and withdrew 800 cc of blood and other fluids. The next morning, when I stopped by, her face was all swollen up. Sores had broken out on her mouth. Apparently, she had contracted herpes. We also thought that perhaps she had gotten a case of mumps since she'd been exposed to some children a few weeks prior to that time. As the day wore on, however, we learned that it wasn't mumps but something probably ten times worse, a massive infection of the parotid gland—the same gland that mumps affects.

A specialist arrived and made a quick diagnosis. "Sadie," he said, "you've got a serious problem. We need to give you penicillin, and you're going to get it in massive doses."

"But, Doctor," Sadie quickly replied, "I can't take penicillin." And with Dr. Jerry, who was familiar with Sadie's medical history nodding his assent, Sadie continued, "I'm allergic to it!"

"But, Sadie, you have to! There's no other way!" the specialist insisted.

"And, if I don't?"

"Well, Sadie, it'll kill you. It's just that simple."

———— **"** ————

Thus, Sadie had been given the choice of dying from a penicillin reaction versus dying from the infection. "I guess one way to go is no worse than the other," Sadie concluded, "God has brought me this far. I'm still in His hand. Bring on the penicillin!"

———— **"** ————

Thus, Sadie had been given the choice of dying from a penicillin reaction versus dying from the infection. "I guess one way to go is no worse than the other," Sadie concluded, "God has brought me this far. I'm still in His hand. Bring on the penicillin!"

Then, with a number of other doctors looking on in disbelief, the specialist wrote out a prescription: four million units of penicillin every three hours.[11]

A bottle of penicillin soon arrived from the pharmacy; the attending nurse quickly connected it to Sadie's IV line. When she had completed this task, instead of returning to the nurses' station, she sat down beside Sadie and engaged herself in some paperwork she had brought with her. I'm not trained in medicine, and the nurse offered no explanation. However, I didn't need one. It didn't take me long to figure out why the nurse sat there.

The penicillin started to flow, drip ... drip ... drip ... and ... there was no reaction! Again, we will probably never know, this side of the "better land," whether the Lord had given the specialist an insight beyond that of his colleagues or had taken what was done and overruled it for good.[12]

———

11   It may have been three million units every four hours. In any case, however, it was a lot.

12   It was some months later that Sadie had an occasion to visit the specialist on another matter. "By the way, Doctor," Sadie began, "I want to thank you for giving me that penicillin. It probably saved my life."

"Don't thank me, Sadie," came his quick reply. "By all the laws of medicine, and with an infection of that magnitude so close to your brain, you should have died anyway! A higher power must have been involved! What I did was merely a last-ditch effort to save an impossible situation."

The day was now drawing to a close. It had been a very hard one for Sadie. In addition to the sores, her mouth was so swollen that it was difficult for her to get her teeth open an eighth of an inch or so to get a drinking straw between them. She had been in a lot of pain; she had told me and her sister several times that day, "I just can't take this anymore. I'm ready to give up and call it quits!" I will never forget how she screamed with pain when I assisted the nurse in trying to move her a few inches in the bed to a more comfortable position.

Late evening came. I had decided to spend the night with her. The nurse found a cot and brought it into her room. After Sadie had finally settled down, I also laid down to see if I could get some sleep. An hour or so later she stirred. Quickly I jumped up to her side. Through clenched teeth she muttered, "I'm gonna lick this thing and get outta here!"

That was the best news I'd heard for some time! An hour later I woke again and looked over to Sadie's direction. To my utter astonishment, Sadie, on her own initiative, was sitting up. Her feet dangled over the edge of the bed. In one hand she had a cup of ice; the other held a spoon. Sadie was feeding herself ice and munching away on it! A few hours earlier she could barely move.

I had just witnessed another miracle!

Chapter 13

Although the immediate crisis had passed, Sadie still had days of pain to endure and sleepless nights. One night, much-needed sleep would not come. Sadie found a pen, a piece of paper, and began to write: Boulder Memorial Hospital, 2 a.m.

"The Lord is my Shepherd." He has many sheep to care for, but He knows me, and gives me special care. I feel secure when He is near me.

"I shall not want." He knows my needs before I ask, and His supply is always more than my wants.

"He maketh me to lie down in green pastures." Sometimes I want to wander where there is no food for my soul. But He knows that I need the green pasture, not only for food, but also for rest and relaxation. There I am reminded of His loving care for me.

"He leads me beside the still waters." I listen to the song of peace in the ripple of the stream. There are no thundering cascades to fill me with fear.

After life's long and strenuous labors, "He restoreth my soul."

"He leads me in the paths of righteousness for His name's sake." They aren't always the paths I would choose to walk, but He knows what is best for me. Sometimes, He must use methods of His choosing, to make me see His way is the best.

There are valleys along the way that are frightening. There is a shadow of death. I know that if He leaves me in such a valley, I cannot make it. But then, I hear the tapping of His rod, and feel His staff gently guiding me, and I fear no evil for I know He is with me, even when I cannot see.

The table He prepares for me is rich in the abundance of the things I need. I feast without fear for I know He prohibits my enemies from stealing that which I need.

He takes time to anoint my head and other wounds with oil. It is soothing. I feel the healing throughout my soul.

With a Shepherd like this, I know that "goodness and mercy shall follow me all the days of my life." He is leading me to a fold where there will be no fear of evil. He wants me to dwell there in peace and happiness. I will listen to His voice each day and follow where He leads. For I do want to "dwell in His house forever."[13]

Then, laying the pen down, Sadie slept until morning.

A few days later, and by what was now becoming a routine, I stopped by the hospital to see her. Then, for the first time in about three weeks, I was able

---

13   Psalm 23.

to "recognize" the girl I had married. Of course, she had been there all along, but because of the massive medications and whatever else, she had undergone a personality shift. Not a major one to be sure and probably unrecognizable by many of her associates, but a shift, nevertheless. At last Sadie's problems had been resolved, or so I thought!

Another day or two elapsed then, on my late afternoon visit, I found her in extreme abdominal pain. What could this possibly mean? Apparently, it was either an inflammation of the pancreas, of which she had a prior history, or perhaps a blocked bowel. With a blood test, the doctor ruled out the pancreas as the source of the problem, so the medical staff concluded the bowel was blocked.

"What does this mean, Dick?" I asked our anesthesiologist friend. "More surgery?"

As a friend, Dick followed Sadie's recovery although he had not been involved on a professional basis. "I'm afraid so, Glenn," he replied. "And, if you like, I will administer the anesthesia."

"I certainly know of no one I'd rather have do it," I responded. "But how much more of this can we expect the poor girl to take?"

"Oh, I think she can probably handle another surgery," Dick reassured me.

But what should I do in the interim? Should I spend another night there in the hospital, or should I go on home and try to get some much-needed rest in order to face the problems I might have to deal with the following day? I finally and reluctantly decided to go home. Needless to say, I was on the telephone early the following morning.

To my great relief, I learned that the bowel obstruction had been relieved via the passageway provided by Mother Nature. Sadie had avoided surgery. Three weeks from the day she had been admitted to the hospital, Sadie came home.

And what had been my thoughts during this time? I am so thankful for the experience of seeing God work out details and experiencing God's peace during Dad's funeral. This time, after I'd recovered from the initial shock and found the time to sit back and evaluate the matter, don't ask me how, *don't ask me how*, but I became convinced that a divine providence was at work and would eventually overrule these events—even if I couldn't understand them at the time.

To me, it was very obvious God had made it possible for me to go to Denmark. *This whole story isn't going to end up in the graveyard!* I thought.

When the doctor said, "Look, we've got a very serious problem here," he might as well have told me, "We've got another valley to cross."

I felt assured that everything was going to be all right. Indeed, later, it came as almost a shock to me when I learned that some people had entertained substantial doubts about Sadie's ultimate recovery.

However, I had found the circumstances puzzling. One day at work, I looked out of my window at the beautiful rock formation called the Flatirons which forms the backdrop for Boulder. I asked God in prayer, "What is going on here anyway? Is this just a bad dream? Is all this really happening?"

And then almost as if a voice from heaven had replied in my thoughts, "Glenn, what have you been praying for during these past months?"

Well, of course. I had been praying that the Lord would give me an experience that would make it possible for me to witness to my family in Denmark. I then recalled a quotation from my favorite author. She had told the story of Jesus healing the two demoniacs after He stilled the waves on Galilee. She followed the story with this comment:

> The two restored demoniacs were the first missionaries whom Christ sent to preach the gospel in the region of Decapolis. For a few moments only these men had been privileged to hear the teachings of Christ. Not one sermon from His lips had ever fallen upon their ears. They could not instruct the people as the disciples who had been daily with Christ were able to do. But they bore in their own persons the evidence that Jesus was the Messiah. *They could tell what they knew; what they themselves had seen, and heard, and felt of the power of Christ.* This is what everyone can do whose heart has been touched by the grace of God.... *As witnesses for Christ, we are to tell what we know, what we ourselves have heard and seen and felt.* If we have been following Jesus step by step, we shall have something right to the point to tell concerning the way in which He has led us. We can tell how we have tested His promise, and found the promise true. We can bear witness to what we have known of the grace of Christ. *This is the witness for which our Lord calls, and for want of which the world is perishing.*[14]

Later that day, or perhaps the next, I briefly stopped by the church on some errand and encountered the pastor's wife. "Roxie," I began, "I think perhaps the Lord has given me this experience in answer to prayer...."

I'll never forget the strange look I received in response. Roxie appeared to not know if she could believe her ears. Could she dismiss what she had just heard as a temporary aberration of the mental state I was in?

---

14   Ellen G. White, *The Desire of Ages* (Mountain View, CA: Pacific Press, 1898), p. 340, emphasis mine.

However, at that point, it all made sense to me. While others may have been concerned about Sadie's recovery, I said to myself, "I have some insights these people don't have. And if I try to explain it, they won't believe me." I just knew that ultimately it was going to be all right! Meanwhile we had received the pathology report on Sadie's tumor. It was benign! In four weeks, we would leave for Denmark.

But then another problem developed. Shortly after Sadie came home from the hospital, I had to make a brief trip to attend some meetings in Washington, D.C. Upon my return, I learned that the approval for my trip to Denmark had been rescinded. Although all of those concerned about my trip had supposedly been consulted, it seemed that someone in the chain of command, and whose signature would be ultimately required, had been overlooked. When the required paperwork had reached his desk, he had said, "Absolutely no way! This won't fly!" And so, we were right back to square one. The problem with the travel ceiling reemerged, even though it had been resolved by describing my trip as a "training assignment."

But I couldn't even get excited about the problem. I just said, "Lord, I know You're going to work this out somehow. I'm just not going to worry about it." I knew I was going.

Chapter 14

At that point, someone back in Washington, a very high official[15] in the National Bureau of Standards, intervened and said, "Look, I think this guy ought to go." Moreover, when the travel allotment had been passed out, he had set some money aside. He said, "I think this is what we ought to use it for." It was just enough to cover my trip.

And so that trip, which by all odds should not have even been allowed, ended up being given a very high priority and at a very high administrative level in Washington. Exactly ten days before we were scheduled to leave, we received approval and the final authorization to go.

We flew to Germany to attend some meetings for a week and then visited a professional colleague at the University of Munich. We also attended the nearby *Passion Play* in Obergamergau. Then we traveled to Skodsborg, the medical institution just north of Copenhagen, Denmark, founded by Dad's uncle, Dr. Carl Ottosen. Here Dad had accepted the Adventist faith.

Agnete and her husband Arne met us in Aalborg. We all wanted to see the house where we would live for the next two months. The availability of this house was probably another miracle which the Lord had worked out in our behalf. Although we didn't realize it at the time, temporary lodging, either a furnished apartment or house, was virtually unavailable in Aalborg—especially during the summertime when many people from Germany come north to take advantage of the miles of pristine beaches surrounding Denmark.

Our host at the university had a "summer house" which would have met our criteria, but it was some fifty or more miles distant and via some rather narrow roads. Hardly an ideal answer. Another professor at Aalborg University provided the solution. He had a comfortable home only a few miles away. He also had another house under construction, out in the country, and at a somewhat greater distance from Aalborg. He would be vacating his current house at about the same time we would need a place. He would be glad to let us use it during our stay.

It didn't take us long to find the spot. Although at one time it had been a schoolhouse, and was well along in years, it was in excellent condition. After a brief examination, Agnete, who had a very comfortable home of her own, remarked, "Look, I think I'd prefer to live here; you can have our house."

---

15 To my regret, I never learned who the official actually was. In my haste to leave, the detail was overlooked. Today it is no doubt buried somewhere in the NBS archives.

In short, it was everything we could possibly want. The back door opened to a beautiful lawn surrounded by a number of different berry bushes and whose fruit would enrich our table in the months to follow. The strawberries were already ripe! A little park adjoined the backyard. It featured a small pond which was the home of some ducks and a pair of swans. A beautiful environment! Although I would ultimately rent an automobile, the path through the park led to the bus stop which provided an alternative way for Sadie to get to town if she wanted.

Just outside the front door and across the street was a little store where we could obtain our basic necessities. Every morning they received a fresh supply of that most delectable item for which the country is noted: Danish pastry! Although we ultimately learned that there would have been a better way, this proved to be a real asset as Sadie struggled to regain some of the weight she had lost as a result of her hospital experience. Moreover, I also indulged in probably more than my share. (The unofficial report was something to the effect that after we left, the local supplier thought that another depression had arrived.)

Some weeks after our arrival, my host's wife and Sadie were out together. During their visit, she said, "Sadie, tell me about your Sabbath...." Sadie thus had an opportunity to witness about God's law, about what He had done for her, and what a loving God we have.

In a short time, I had settled into a routine at the university. I was anxious to renew my acquaintance with Jorgen Anderson, the gentleman whom I'd met on the airplane approximately two years earlier. He been on vacation when I arrived but now, we arranged to meet. During our visit, I told him a bit more about my interest in Denmark and about Dad's court-martial, which had probably taken place within a mile of the place where we held our conversation.

"Glenn, that's quite a story," he commented when I had finished. "It may have been reported in the local newspaper. Maybe you should go down there and see if you can find out more about it."

"Newspaper?? You ... you mean they published newspapers back then?"

My host smiled broadly. "Glenn, you've forgotten that this is Europe! That newspaper has been published for the past 250 years. We're talking about a recent event!"

The next day during my noon hour, I made my way down to the newspaper office. After explaining my errand, they quickly granted me access to their archives. Moreover, a pleasant young lady, of one of their reporters, soon arrived to assist in my search. The problem, however, was that except for a six-month time frame, I didn't know when the court-martial had taken place. We started to look, but it quickly became apparent that we were looking for the proverbial needle in a haystack.

"Let me try the military archives," the reporter suggested.

"That has been tried," I replied. "I don't think it will work." I then explained to the reporter that several years earlier, I'd had some correspondence with someone in Denmark who had learned of Dad's story. He had somehow obtained my name and address and wanted to learn more about it. In response I had suggested that he try the Danish military archives. In due time, he had reported back that the archives couldn't be opened until eighty years after the event. At that time, about ten years remained.

Because then it was past time for me to go back to work, we parted.

Several days later, however, upon my return home, Sadie met me. "The newspaper reporter called. They got your dad's military records!"

Needless to say, I went back to the newspaper office the next day! It is not possible to put into words how I felt when the reporter handed me the documents she had procured and which she explained to me. Although I had been familiar with the story since childhood, she recreated it before my very eyes! There, just as Dad told it, he was charged with disobeying orders on the drill field. In addition, he had "disobeyed the rules and regulations about being in his quarters at night."[16] Then came the disposition of the court-martial sentence, "Pardoned by the King!"

After I had partially recovered from my state of thought, the reporter continued, "Now we'd like to do a story on this, and we will want to get your picture!"

At that point I started thinking rather furiously. "Let's … let's wait a little bit," I responded. "I'm really not dressed for that right now. That story has been there for seventy years, a few more days isn't going to hurt anything…."

In reality, I had something else in mind. In view of their adherence to the Lutheran faith, it had occurred to me that, initially at least, the court-martial may well have been an embarrassment to the family in Denmark.

Upon returning home, I immediately got in touch with my cousin, Peter. If anyone spoke for Aunt Emma and the rest of the family in Denmark, he

---

16 At one time, during his brief military career in Aalborg, Dad had made the mistake of setting his watch by the clock at the train station, which apparently was five minutes slow. He had been visiting his girlfriend that evening and upon returning to his military station, he was five minutes late. Upon learning of this "offense," he had been informed by his commanding officer that, in addition to violating the orders on the drill field, he was to be charged with "violation of the rules and regulations pertaining to his being in his quarters at night." Thus, his punishment was to be all the greater. Apparently, Dad's commanding officer had followed through on his word!

probably did. After relating what had happened, I told him of the proposed story and of my probable role in it.

"I'm proud of my family here in Denmark," I continued, "but this story is going to be printed, and they are going to mention me, of course, and I would like to have it include my family here. Before I do so, I want to know how you feel about this whole thing and of its possibly including the family in Denmark."

As I had anticipated, Peter quickly assured me that there was "no problem."

Several days later, I was back at the newspaper office, and they took pictures. After we finished with the photographer, I said to the reporter, "Do you have a few more minutes?"

"Certainly," she replied. "I have time for whatever you have in mind."

"Well, first of all I want to thank you. I can't begin to tell you what this experience has meant to me. It has been one of the most moving ones of my entire life. I only wish that Dad could have lived to have seen this day. But you know," I continued, "there's a better land. I'm planning on meeting my father there, and this will be one of the first things I will want to share with him! I … I hope you're planning on being there too!"

And she thanked me.

Chapter 15

A few days later the Aalborg newspaper, which carries the name *Aalborg Stiftstidende*, ran a feature article which carried the headline:
"Court-martialed in 1910, Steadfast Soldier Goes to Prison for His Beliefs."

And the article continued:

A young man from Elling, near Frederickshavn, Oskar [Oscar] Christensen, who served his duty as a soldier at Aalborg, was shortly after induction court-martialed and given a hard prison sentence because he, for religious reasons, would not work on Saturdays. The case took place in 1910, and it got a happy ending. Oskar Christensen had his punishment remitted by a pardon from King Frederick the Eighth.

Shortly after completing his military service, Oskar Christensen emigrated to America, and the case of the strong principled man from Vendsussel, [a province in northern Denmark] became, among the residents of North Jutland, a forgotten book. So it would have remained had not a son of Oskar Christensen, who, in the United States took the last name, Engen, after his native farm, a short time ago, asked Aalborg Stiftstidende, for assistance in establishing the precise date of the event.[17]

From there the article said that Oskar Engen's youngest son, Glenn Engen, had visited North Jutland numerous times. It then portrayed me as a "distinguished international scientist"[18] who was being hosted by their local university. In conjunction with the other professors, I was working on a six-port, an idea on which I held a patent in the United States. I was associated with the National Bureau of Standards. The article then made mention of the rest of my family connections there in Denmark. In conclusion, it gave a brief synopsis of *Vikingsonnen* (the Danish translation of *Son of the Vikings*, Josephine Cunnington Edwards' book about my father) and indicated that it was available in book form.

Then came the picture showing me focused on my father's military records. The story's climax, however, came in the caption under the picture:

---

17   Aalborg Stiftstidende. Fredag 8 August, 1980 (translated from Danish).
18   The reader is, of course, familiar with the Master's words to the effect that, "a prophet is without honor in his own country" (Mark 6:4, paraphrase). In my experience, the other side of this coin is something to the effect that one's reputation increases in direct proportion to his distance from his place of work. Thus, a "distinguished international scientist" is merely one who happens to be in a foreign country.

"Glenn Engen is the Youngest Son of Oskar Engen *and He Shares His Father's Faith.*"[19]

And thus, in an environment where there was little belief in a personal God, and least of all in the scientific community, I had been given the opportunity to witness to the newspaper's readers, which numbered in the thousands, to the faith which I hold dear.

A few days later we visited the home of Anna, Dad's cousin in Frederickshavn. She had been barely into her teens at the time of the court-martial. The interest with which that dear lady devoured the content of the newspaper article was a sight to behold.

> ❝
> *Glenn Engen is the Youngest Son of Oskar Engen and He Shares His Father's Faith.*
> ❞

But there was another reader for whom the story was of more than casual interest. Carla was living in Aalborg. As she came across the name of her great uncle, Carl Ottosen, she immediately recognized that she was related to the individuals in the story. To her disappointment, the local library was unable[20] to provide a copy of *Vikingsonnen*. She then turned to her telephone directory and started looking for the names of the others in Denmark mentioned in the article. We were soon in contact and arranged a meeting. As it worked out, my sister, Ruth, and her husband, Bob, arrived from Loma Linda, California, for a brief visit a few hours before our scheduled meeting. Thus, we had the pleasure of becoming acquainted with a second cousin of whose existence we had been unaware. Before parting, she had a copy of *Vikingsonnen*.

---

19   Aalborg Stiftstidende, Fredag 8 August, 1980 (translated from Danish) emphasis mine.
20   A few days later, I paid the library a visit and provided them with a copy.

Chapter 16

Our sojourn in Denmark was rapidly coming to a close. Ruth and Bob had timed their arrival so that after spending a few days with us in Denmark, we could join them in an automobile trip to Norway. Our first day was uneventful, but the second morning out, and after a delightful stay at a "bed and breakfast" in Sweden, I diverted my attention from the road and looked at Sadie.

I immediately recognized that she was in trouble. She was in big trouble! She appeared to be deathly ill and was experiencing severe abdominal pain! As soon as we could, we drove to a small clinic on the south side of Oslo which provided hydrotherapy and related therapies. Although hardly meeting the criteria for emergency care, we hoped their staff could at least direct us to the appropriate resources for dealing with Sadie's problem.

Unfortunately, their beds were totally occupied by other guests, and the head of their medical staff was not immediately available. However, they graciously gave us the use of a couch in a small lounge. Although Sadie was now able to lie down, the fierce pain continued unabated. An hour or so later, their doctor came in.

He did a quick assessment. "She needs to get to a hospital," he immediately said.

"Shall we take her by our car?" I asked.

"No, I'm sending for an ambulance," he replied.

Needless to say, many prayers had ascended to heaven in the interim. Sadie had a good talk with the Lord. What could her problem possibly be? Was our trip to Norway to terminate at the hospital? Was Sadie going to require surgery?

The doctor called and the ambulance was on its way. Before its arrival, however, and almost as quickly as it had developed, most of Sadie's pain disappeared. When the ambulance arrived, she was able to walk to it, rather than being transported on a gurney as we had anticipated. Soon we arrived at the hospital. They ran numerous tests, but the hospital staff couldn't find anything wrong. By the next morning, the pain was gone. Her condition appeared to be stable, and we continued our trip. But what had happened?

Too many times we ask the Lord to answer our prayers and then, when He does, we try to explain it by natural means. Maybe she had a gas bubble or something like that. But it wasn't. The pain was too severe for that.

I believe that possibly the Lord had given us this experience for another reason. Although my university colleagues had been impressed by the newspaper article, up to that time I'd not had the chance to say much to them on the subject of religion. I had wanted to witness to them but really didn't know quite how. But they and many others were well aware of what Sadie had been through prior to our arrival in Denmark. Upon our return from Norway they asked, "And how did Sadie tolerate the trip?"

I then related what had happened and added a few additional words, "You know, when life's going easy, everything is going fine, too many times we think we can get along without religion. But in a situation like that, we really find out if our religion means anything to us. I don't know your background, but just let me tell you, if you don't know my Jesus, you're missing an awful lot!"

All too soon it was time to leave Aalborg. Ruth and Bob had rented a car in Copenhagen, obtained some camping equipment, and planned to continue their tour of Europe. We planned to stop briefly in Copenhagen and then fly to Warsaw where I would attend a microwave conference. After leaving the conference, we would go to Frankfurt where I had reserved a small motor home. We also would tour southern Germany and Switzerland—in style!

Some weeks had now elapsed since the newspaper story, but in the interim, I had been led to wonder if perhaps there was more of Dad's story in the military archives. I determined to find out during our stay in Copenhagen. Initially, I planned to go to the military archives by myself, but the Lord saw to it that I was accompanied by a Danish friend who was also a professional colleague. With his help, we were soon in touch with a member of the military staff.

"And what religion are you?" he demanded.

I was completely taken aback by the brusque response to my inquiry. "Well, I … I'm also a Seventh-day Adventist," I managed to stammer.

"He's not here to make trouble," my Danish colleague intervened, talking to the one in charge of the archives. "He's not going to conduct a postmortem on the court-martial or anything like that. He's only interested in learning more about the story."

The archivist's demeanor changed a little. When he learned that Dr. Carl Ottosen was involved, whom he had known personally, this really broke the ice.

"I'll take your name and address," he said. "I'll see what I can do, but I can't make any promises."

After attending the meeting in Warsaw and picking up the camper in Frankfurt, we soon enjoyed the marvelous scenery in Switzerland. Our preferred method of touring Europe has always been by private automobile. With our self-contained camper, we didn't even need to look for a place to stay at night. All we needed was a level place to park with an occasional stop at a campground to obtain a fresh supply of water and take care of our waste disposal. Thus, we happened to be at a campground in southern Switzerland one evening.

I emerged from a restroom, and to my surprise, I saw my sister Ruth and her husband Bob. We compared notes and learned that the idea of meeting had occurred to both of us when we had visited in Denmark, but we both dismissed it as impractical because of the problem of communicating with each other while we were both in motion. And now it had happened entirely by accident! Or was it an accident? Who could calculate the odds on that?

Actually, we had been to the campground earlier that day to renew our water supply and only returned because we couldn't find a comfortable place to park. Moreover, the campground was so large that we could have both easily been there without ever seeing one another. Rather than an "accident," I would like to believe that God was looking down with a smile on His face and saying to Himself, "They haven't asked for this, but I have prepared a little surprise for them.…" In any case, I quickly found Sadie and told her to set two extra places on our supper table. Although we had separate itineraries for the next day or two, before parting we had settled on another meeting place and spent the following weekend together in Grindenwald.

Thus ended our trip to Europe. It had certainly been a rewarding one, both on a personal as well as professional level. For all I knew, that was the end of the story. But God had other plans.

Chapter 17

Six weeks after returning home, to my surprise, I received a large packet in the mail—more of Dad's military record. There, in complete agreement with Dad's recollection, was a roster of the thirteen officers who had participated in the court-martial. I leafed through another couple of pages to read a summary of the background investigation which had taken place. A letter from the Scandinavian Union Conference outlined the biblical basis for keeping the seventh-day Sabbath and its author had concluded with parallel words to Luther's defense before the Diet of Worms: "Here we stand. We cannot do otherwise!"[21]

Then, I found a letter from Dad's uncle, Dr. Carl Ottosen, who noted that Dad's mother had died from tuberculosis and that it was quite possible that Dad had a similar "weakness." Perhaps the court-martial would take this into consideration in reaching a decision as to the nature and extent of Dad's punishment.

Then I found another document—something looked strangely familiar. What was it? Was it the handwriting? Although my knowledge of Danish was still very limited, I was able to decipher a few of the key words. The bottom was signed by "Recruit #78." I then realized that the document in my hands was a Xerox copy of the letter that Dad, himself, had written while in prison, and in his own behalf, explaining to the military authorities his position on Sabbath observance.

Although the story provided by the military archives agreed with Dad's account down to some very small details, there was also a significant difference, and which, in the interests of accuracy, should be noted. According to the military version, there was no evidence to suggest that Dad had been sentenced to anything other than three weeks of "simple prison" on bread and water. Not a pleasant prospect to be sure but certainly far short of imprisonment for life, which had been Dad's understanding. So, how does one reconcile the two accounts? After a review of the available evidence, I have concluded that the "three weeks" was, indeed, the court-martial sentence; the rest was merely a threat. It may have been enlarged upon by the one who conveyed the message to him in an effort to see if they could crush his resolve.

But does this really alter the story? I, at least, think not. To be more specific, in my opinion, my dad needs to be remembered for his adherence to his faith in the face of what he believed would be the ultimate consequences of his decision, rather than, and apart from the pardon, what might have actually evolved from it.

---

21   Scandinavian Union Conference. Personal letter (translated from the Danish original).

Chapter 18

A few years following this trip, the Technical University of Denmark, located a few miles north of Copenhagen, granted me another brief tenure as a visiting professor in Scandinavia. During this time, we had the opportunity of visiting Dansk Bogforlag, the SDA Danish publishing house in Odense. After spending the night there, we were asked to join their staff the following morning for their worship service. Thus, we again had the opportunity of again sharing Sadie's experience in the hospital.

Although Copenhagen was not as convenient to our family in North Jutland, Denmark is a small country, and Sadie and I spent many weekends visiting Agnete, Aunt Emma, and Dad's cousin, Anna. Unfortunately, in the interim, Agnete had developed cancer and was taking chemotherapy.

One of the most difficult farewells we have ever experienced was our parting with Agnete when my tenure expired. By all the laws of medicine, we would never see her again, and that's the way it happened. I find great comfort, however, in the belief which she expressed in her last letter to me, namely, that we would see each other again in that "better land."

In time, Sadie's story was written and published in a monthly worldwide evangelistic journal. Aunt Emma, of course, was quite interested and had shared this story with a number of her friends. Some time later, we again visited her. In the interim, Agnete had died. Sadie and Aunt Emma were discussing the story and Sadie had concluded with, "I really don't know why God was so good to me."

Without hesitation Aunt Emma replied, "Well, Sadie, I know. Neta [Agnete] needed you."

Chapter 19

On Friday, October 13, 1995, our lives changed dramatically. We had spent the previous several months in North Carolina with Sadie's brother, Jim, who was terminally ill with cancer. His funeral had been held in Detroit, where he had spent the major portion of his life. After attending the funeral, we had traveled 120 miles to the home of some friends who live outside of Battle Creek, Michigan. We had planned to meet my brother, sister, and their respective spouses for a mini family reunion.

We arrived about 9 p.m. By mutual understanding, our friends had all gone to a meeting and had not returned yet. I was backing our fifth wheel trailer into their driveway; Sadie was outside with a flashlight giving me directions. Because my eyes were focused on the rearview mirrors, I never saw the oncoming vehicle. Apparently, the driver was either stoned or drunk and at the last moment recognized that she was on a collision course with me. Although she had ample room to have passed by me on the other side of the road, for unknown reasons she took to the shallow ditch, missed my truck by inches, then hit and bounced along the side of the trailer, which was now well into the driveway.

Seeing the flash go by and hearing the thud, I quickly realized that the trailer been hit. Jumping from the truck, I quickly ran to the back of the trailer and scanned the area where Sadie had been standing. But where was she?

Quickly looking around, I saw a flashlight some distance away. Running as fast as I could, I found her there, lying on her back, her legs bent at right angles to her side. Sadie had apparently been transported some forty or more feet on the hood of the other car and then thrown off! Because of the sounds she was making, I knew she was alive! The force with which she had been struck was such that the zipper on her jacket had left an imprint on the bumper of the offending vehicle! But … Sadie was alive!

> **"**
> *Quickly looking around, I saw a flashlight some distance away. Running as fast as I could, I found her there, lying on her back, her legs bent at right angles to her side. Sadie had apparently been transported some forty or more feet on the hood of the other car and then thrown off!*
> **"**

The car had come to a stop about fifteen feet away; its front door was open. The driver, a woman forty-plus years of age, who apparently was not wearing a seat belt, was on the passenger side.

"Are you hurt?" I asked the woman.

"No," she replied. "Was anyone else hurt?"

"Yes, my wife. Will you come and stay with her while I call the ambulance?"

Slowly she emerged from her vehicle. I bolted for the front door of the nearby house, fully expecting to find it locked and wondering which window I would have to break in order to gain an entrance....

I turned the doorknob—and walked in.

I later learned that, indeed, the door had been locked. Moreover, because my sister's husband Bob had been the last one to leave the house, my sister, Ruth, had requested of the lady who owned the house, "Could you please double check to make certain that the door is securely locked?"

The owner had checked, and the door had been locked.

Yet the instant I touched the knob, and with no effort on my part, the door swung wide open....

It was almost as if there had been someone inside who had seen my approach and had opened it for me. But no one was inside. In the days which followed, I had occasion to use that door a number of times. It was fitted with weather stripping and, as is common with such doors, required a nominal "push" to open it.

I quickly located the telephone and dialed 911. "I need an ambulance!!"

"Where are you?" the dispatcher asked.

"Yes. Where am I?" I paused. "Let's see, I'm somewhere south of that little town. What was its name? Am I in Ceresco?"

"Yes. But what is the name of the street or road?"

I had the directions written on a slip of paper; they were somewhat involved, and the paper was still in the truck. In my stress, I could not recall them.

"What is the house number?"

"I can't tell you."

"Could you go outside and look?"

I did, but then I decided to let the driver of the other vehicle talk to the operator while I stayed with Sadie. I looked for her. While I had been calling, she had driven off![22] Sadie was still crying. "I hurt! Please help me! Oh, dear Lord, please help me!! I hurt!!"

---

22   It took the police one week to locate the other driver, and she was sentenced to three years' probation, to be followed by a year in jail if she violated its fairly stringent terms. She was indigent and had neither

Leaving her side, I ran inside the trailer to get a pillow. Although well aware that one does not move an injured person who is unconscious, I was unsure if the same guidelines applied in the present situation. In any case, for better or worse, I gently lifted her head and placed the pillow under it, while watching for any signs of additional stress or pain. I then had to decide whether to stay with Sadie and try to comfort her during what, to all indications, may have been her dying moments or complete my 911 call. After wrestling for some moments with my heart, my head prevailed, but never has it been harder to say "no" to my heart.

Meanwhile, the dispatcher had put a tracer on the telephone, and an ambulance was already on its way. We later learned that a member of the area's "first response unit" lived less than a mile away. He'd had his scanner on, had heard my 911 call, and in spite of my garbled response to the operator, had deduced that I was close by.

As I emerged from the house, the ambulance was already on the scene. An EMT put in an IV, and the attendants attempted to straighten Sadie's badly mangled legs. Then, in order to make an initial assessment of the extent of her injuries, while avoiding a possible exacerbation of them, the female member of the ambulance crew started cutting up the leg of Sadie's slacks with a pair of scissors.

As I looked on, the police officer, who had also been summoned and who apparently had been waiting for this time, appeared and wanted to see the vehicle registration, etcetera. My attention was thus diverted from the awkward and revealing procedure.

Soon the EMTs put Sadie on the gurney and loaded her into the ambulance. But where were they going to take her? The larger hospital in Battle Creek was farther away; the ambulance had come from Marshall. I had been busy talking with the police officer and had not been able to follow the course of events. Fortunately, indeed providentially, my sister and the rest of the family had returned in the interim to find their front yard occupied with emergency vehicles and flashing lights.

When Ruth learned that the ambulance planned to take her to Marshall, she immediately asked, "Is Battle Creek an option?"

"Yes, we can take her there."

I readily gave my approval.

As it turned out, not only would the facilities of the better-equipped hospital be severely taxed in the days and weeks to follow, but the location was

---

a valid driver's license nor automobile license. However, Sadie's medical bills, both for the past (which now total more than $600,000) and for the future, were covered for life by our own insurance.

much more convenient to the trailer park where I and others would be staying. Moreover, Battle Creek was the place where I had spent much of my childhood and completed my secondary education. Although more than four decades had elapsed since it had been "home" to me, there were still familiar faces and friends.

With the destination settled, the ambulance was soon on its way. My family and I would follow. Before leaving, however, I remembered those who had been at the funeral in Detroit. Many of them would want to know about the accident but they were mostly from out of town and staying in motels. But where? How could I reach them?

I then thought of John, from North Carolina, who had attended the funeral. He had been a long-time friend of the deceased's family, first during the time they had lived in Detroit and more recently after their move to North Carolina. Perhaps he was staying with his brother who lived in Detroit and who was an acquaintance of ours. I quickly made a telephone call.

"Is John staying with you, by any chance?"

"No, he is not. But I have a phone number where you can reach him."

In a few minutes I was in touch with John, had told him about the accident, and left him to deal with the problem as best he could. We heard the story later.

John was ready to start informing people as soon as I hung up, but where or how should he start? He then remembered that Alice, the widow of the deceased, had a brother who worked at a police station in Detroit. Perhaps he would know where Alice was staying. Looking up a list of the Detroit police stations, John prepared to call them one by one. An officer answered his first call.

"Do you by any chance know an Art Umlauf?"

"Certainly," the officer replied. "He's sitting at the desk next to me. Would you like to talk to him?"

John's first call had reached Alice's brother! Moreover, he knew where Alice was staying and she, in turn, knew where the rest were. Thus, the problem of informing the others about Sadie's tragedy was quickly resolved.

My family and I were soon at the hospital. There, a social worker met us and stayed with us well into the early morning hours, certainly well beyond his normal tour of duty. He stayed to render all possible assistance in helping us deal with what appeared to be the probable loss of our loved one. After providing some routine information to the clerk at the admitting desk, hospital staff ushered us into the small chapel to await the medical evaluation. We waited several hours. In the interim, our son, David, arrived from Detroit. Eventually the doctor appeared to give us his assessment:

"I don't know what other medical problems she may have had," he began, "but this is far worse than anything she may have had before. It is probably worse than all of her prior problems put together … she may not survive…."

Sadie's knees were so badly mangled that the only thing holding them together was the skin. Her pelvis was broken in addition to her femur, wrist, ribs, and more. Although, if taken individually, these probably would not have been life threatening, the trauma associated with their simultaneous occurrence might well prove to be more than her body could handle.

But, in spite of the force with which she had been struck, there had been no internal, back, or head injuries. Surely this was another of the many miracles to follow.

Upon hearing his assessment, I started to protest, "But, Doctor, I know something about that girl you don't know!" I started to relate how God had intervened in her prior surgery.

Because the doctor had more pressing responsibilities, he did not have time to hear me out. Were her present problems really more life threatening than that? Perhaps. My mind then went back to another story, one she had shared with me while we were courting….

Chapter 20

"I don't care what you signed! If that child dies, you're going to sue that _____ _____ hospital for every nickel they've got!!"

The words had been spoken to Sadie's parents and in a room adjoining the one where she was lying in bed. At the time, Sadie was ten years of age. Ten days earlier she had been accompanying her father on what had started as a routine errand. Their car had been sideswiped by another vehicle. Sadie had been thrown out, had landed on her head and fractured her skull on the streetcar track. Upon reaching the emergency room, the staff, who were busy with other accident victims, had made a quick evaluation:

"She's dead; take her on to the morgue!"

Before these instructions could be carried out, however, Sadie's father had intervened. He was a policeman and had overheard the conversation. He had brought many accident victims to the emergency room and was well known by the head doctor.

> **Please. Please! Can't you do anything to save my little girl? Try anything!!**

"Please. Please! Can't you do anything to save my little girl? Try anything!!"

And so, the head doctor had intervened in what to all appearances was a hopeless situation.

In disgust, those who were directly involved in her care had put in a few stitches and sent her up to the ward. She could die there. They hadn't even taken the time to apply an antiseptic or remove the dirt embedded in her wound.[23]

Some days later Sadie recovered consciousness, but it soon became apparent that her care was rather low on the hospital's priority list. In the interim, the "police doctor," who was under contract with the city of Detroit to provide medical care to its officers, had learned of Sadie's condition. At his prompting, Sadie's parents elected to take her home. Although Sadie's care to this point could probably be characterized by little more than "indifference," the hospital staff now became alarmed. Before regaining the custody of their daughter, Sadie's parents had been required to sign numerous forms indicating that they would accept full responsibility for her "impending death."

---

23   Quite obviously, this was in the days before "malpractice suits" were the order of the day.

For some days, Sadie lapsed in and out of consciousness. Then, following a torrent of profanity, the likes of which her tender ears had never before heard, came those words from the police doctor: "If that child dies...."

"Die? Who's going to die? Me?? I don't want to die!! I want to live! I want to grow up and be a teacher so I can tell other boys and girls about Jesus and His love."

And so, Sadie promised Jesus that if her life was spared, she would be a witness for Him.

Surely the injuries which Sadie had just sustained were not as bad as that had been! On the other hand, that had been more than six decades ago, and her body's restorative abilities had no doubt diminished with time. In any case, there had been prior miracles in her life. For better or worse, she was in God's hand. Would He, in His infinite wisdom and compassion, again see fit to intervene? Only time would tell.

Chapter 21

It had taken several hours to assemble the surgeons and other specialists who would now take control. We were later advised, by one who was in a position to know, that a better team would have been hard to find. Because her knees had been so badly mangled, the initial assessment was that her lower legs would have to be amputated. But no, after making the appropriate incisions the surgeon discovered, to his delight, that the all-important blood vessels were still intact! Initially at least, the amputation could wait!

The ligaments, those all-important bands of tissue which hold the knee "together," however, presented another problem. In the left knee, all of these had been torn loose. One of the four could be reattached but in the absence of the other three, and the resulting loss in stability, would the lower leg become merely a useless appendage? Maybe the knee would heal in such a way that the leg would be completely stiff. Given the circumstances, this was the best possible outcome the surgeon dared hope for.

The prognosis for the right leg was a little better. Here the femur had been broken in two places. As a consequence, the injury to the knee joint was less severe. With the help of a metal insert, the femur would heal in time. Only one of the ligaments had been torn loose and that could be reattached.

It was five in the morning before the physicians had completed the most urgent surgery. They would do additional surgery the following day. The night had been exhausting for all of us.

For the first few days, Sadie made remarkable progress in her recovery. She had been transferred from the intensive care unit and was on the surgical floor. However, because of the trauma she had suffered, her immune system was down, and she got pneumonia and a staph infection. When her breathing became labored, the hospital immediately returned her to intensive care and put her on a "ventilator," or breathing machine.

Although she was only semiconscious at the time, Sadie's body considered the ventilator an "insult." In order to secure her "cooperation," medical staff had to put Sadie into a "medically induced" coma and then had to give her medication which would temporarily paralyze her lungs. Thus, Sadie became totally dependent on the ventilator for her next breath. The tube which supplied the air to her lungs was initially placed via her mouth, although later the tube went through a tracheotomy.

Although she was now in a coma, at one point Sadie bit down on this tube, shutting off her air supply. This precipitated a major alarm on the ward. Nurses shoved me out the door, as staff came from all directions to deal with the impending crisis. Great was their relief when they found that the immediate problem was not serious.

However, the available antibiotics for dealing with her particularly vicious staph infection were hard on the kidneys and for about two or more weeks she experienced kidney failure. The doctors had to walk a tightrope between restoring the function of her lungs and pushing her kidneys over the edge. Because of fluid retention, her pre-hospital weight of perhaps 125 pounds almost reached 180 pounds! Her head was little more than a knob on top of a grossly inflated torso. Her neck had completely disappeared. Her legs and thighs had swollen to twice their normal size.

Unfortunately, the hospital did not have a dialysis facility; it was more than twenty miles to the nearest place where this was available. Sadie would need to be transported by helicopter. But, given her condition, was this even an option?

The fever raged on for days. In order to keep it from becoming completely out of control, at times she had to be covered by a special type of blanket through which cold water could be circulated. Her nostrils were filled with caked blood.

Although the coma had been initiated by the medical staff, it persisted well beyond the intended time. For the first three weeks, Sadie's eyes were closed; another two weeks followed with her eyes partially open but with nothing behind them other than a blank stare. The staff started to wonder if she had experienced internal head injuries which had gone undetected during the initial evaluation. Moreover, there had been a substantial drop in the oxygen level in her blood prior to her having been connected to the ventilator. Had the oxygen drop damaged her brain?

In the immediate aftermath of the accident, and for several weeks thereafter, Sadie's sister Lella and a niece Sharon stayed on and maintained a "round the clock" vigil at the hospital. Following this, my sister Ruth and her husband Bob returned from their California home to stay with me and await the outcome. I found a trailer park five miles from the hospital and moved our trailer there.

Our daily routine had evolved. Ruth and I would get up early and arrive at the hospital in time to see the doctors during their morning rounds. Then we would go back to the trailer where Bob would have breakfast ready. Following this, I would drop them off at the local senior center while I returned to the hospital. After rejoining them for lunch, we did other chores. After supper, when weather and road conditions permitted, I would then make a third trip to the hospital to check on Sadie's progress.

Over the years Sadie had been hospitalized on numerous occasions, some of which were also life threatening. In this context I had come to accept the premise that the attending staff must, of necessity, treat the patient with a certain amount of "professional detachment." After all, if one permitted oneself to become personally involved with every potential tragedy one encounters in an ICU environment, one would soon become a physical and emotional wreck.

However, I saw no evidence of this "detachment." By contrast, I doubt that the staff could have shown more loving interest and concern had it been their own mother who was there on the life support systems and skillfully medicated and managed by the doctors and nurses. I doubt that she could have received more personal attention had she been the only patient in their care.

It had now been approximately six weeks since the accident. For the past five weeks she had been in the coma. During my solo trips to the hospital, I had derived great comfort from a recently acquired tape featuring the musical voice of Dick Barron and those all-comforting words, "Jesus will walk with me down thru the valley. ... I know He will walk with me."[24]

I had several talks with God, and told Him in essence that, although my choice would be that it might continue a bit longer, I had spent more than forty wonderful years with Sadie. If, in His all-seeing providence, her untimely death would eventually result in others being in heaven, who otherwise would not make it, I would "give her back" to Him....

Every day Sadie survived was now a major milestone. Indeed, I was beginning to wonder if we were depriving Sadie of the right to "die in peace and with dignity." Every day I anticipated that the medical staff would tell me that the time had come to "pull the plug." And had they done so, I was prepared to accept their decision without protest. Plans for her funeral were in preparation.

By this time few, if any, of the attending staff expected Sadie to survive. Although our son David had returned to his home in California, he made routine phone calls during the night to the nursing station. He kept his own chart to monitor her progress. After obtaining the results from the tests of interest, he would then ask the nurse to give her own personal assessment of Sadie's condition.

On one night in particular, after a long pause, the nurse said, "Quite frankly, I don't know why we're doing this [to her]...."

---

24   Haldor Lillenas. "Jesus will Walk with Me down through the Valley." Hymnary.org, https://1ref.us/238. Accessed September 23, 2022.

Chapter 22

Then, on a never-to-be-forgotten day, I arrived at the hospital. For some reason Ruth was not with me that morning. Although Sadie's eyes had been open for the past two weeks, something about them appeared to be different.

"Do you know what?" I asked, beginning a little word game we had frequently shared.

Slowly Sadie shook her head.

"Well! You're a dummy!!" I continued in mock disgust. The answer was that I loved her.

Slowly the corners of her mouth fell, a look of frustration, disappointment, and sorrow crossed her face.

I quickly reassured her. "Of course, I love you!"

Because of her tracheotomy, Sadie had been unable to respond verbally, *but she was responding! After six long weeks she was able to communicate with me via that mischievous grin and captivating smile of hers, even if she was unable to talk. We were communicating again!!*

Back at the trailer I had to tell someone. Who? My thoughts immediately turned to our son, David. It was 4:30 a.m. in California, but I couldn't wait. Upon reaching him I managed to stammer, "It's … it's a miracle.…" but then choked up.

> **Then, on a never-to-be-forgotten day, I arrived at the hospital. For some reason Ruth was not with me that morning. Although Sadie's eyes had been open for the past two weeks, something about them appeared to be different.**

Only a few hours had elapsed since he had heard that evaluation from the nursing station, "I don't know why we're doing this." My words hardly matched the message he was dreading, but had he heard them correctly? Great was his relief when I was able to continue.

Little by little, Sadie's kidneys started to resume their function. It was a banner day when they put out more fluid, on a daily basis, than she took in via the IVs. At one time there had been a dozen or more IVs going simultaneously. Following this, she made gradual progress, although weaning her from the ventilator took time. Her initial resistance to the machine had turned into a love affair! For a number of weeks, she took two steps forward, then one or one-and-a-half steps backward. Gradually, ever so gradually, the muscles in her lungs had to be coaxed back into taking over. During the interim, the muscles in her arms had gone into a state of atrophy because of disuse. Her leg injuries were far from healed. She was little more than a paraplegic. But she was getting better! It was a major event when she was able to lift her arm from the bed and touch her nose.

By mid-December (1995) Sadie was becoming more alert. But what would her reactions be when she recovered to the point where she realized where she had been for the past two months? Although there were still months of rehabilitation ahead, hopefully her need for hospital care would soon come to an end. What should we do next?

There was an excellent rehabilitation facility near our home in Boulder, perhaps the best in the entire state of Colorado. One by one, as the opportunity presented itself, I approached her doctors, telling them about the facility and its proximity to our home.

"Should we try to transport her there by air ambulance? Would this meet the approval of the medical staff? Would the insurance company pay for this?"

Only one doctor thought we should perhaps first wait to see "if she survived." The rest gave the idea guarded approval. Yes, the cost would be covered by our insurance, although at that point I had concluded that, if necessary, I would pay it from my own pocket.

Another week or two elapsed before we could complete the necessary arrangements and her physicians felt she was well enough to make the trip. Since I would also be going along in the air ambulance, our nephew Dan volunteered to come and drive our truck and trailer back to Colorado. Our immediate destination was Avista Hospital, the Adventist facility serving the Boulder area and the hospital where Sadie had been serving as a volunteer chaplain.

On December 21, 1995, medical staff wheeled Sadie's gurney to an air ambulance. I followed the gurney and entered the plane. We took off from Battle Creek, Michigan, and headed for Boulder, Colorado, our home, landing in Broomfield, Colorado, the closest airport to the hospital. Sadie's room at Avista Hospital had been decorated with Christmas greenery, lights, and colored balls, including the words, "Welcome home, Sadie!!" For me, a guest room awaited at the home of some dear friends.

At Avista, Sadie would be under the care of an orthopedic surgeon, also a personal friend. The orthopedist had also arranged for a colleague of his to evaluate and oversee Sadie's continuing need for pulmonary therapy. We later learned that when the pulmonary specialist initially evaluated Sadie, he did not expect her to survive—even at that point in her recovery.

However, after two additional weeks, Sadie finally said "farewell" to the ventilator. She was ready for transfer to the Mapleton Rehabilitation Facility. Meanwhile, our trailer had arrived from Michigan. There was a full hookup available only a few hundred feet from the front door of the rehabilitation center and within sight of the room where Sadie would be staying. At the time of her admission, she still needed assistance from at least three and preferably four people just to get out of bed. Moreover, after ten or more weeks in bed, she had yet to learn to tolerate being in a vertical position, to say nothing about being able to stand.

But slowly, ever so slowly, she responded to the therapy. With the aid of a walker, she could take a few steps. Her left knee, which had been more badly injured than the other one, could be stabilized with the help of a brace. After two months of rehabilitation, she could get out of bed, go to the bathroom, and do other things by herself. Although her primary means of locomotion would continue to be a wheelchair, she no longer needed the twenty-four-hour care of the rehabilitation center.

At the time of her discharge, the staff gave Sadie a "going away" party. They told her that of all the patients who had come through that facility, she had made the most progress—and in the least amount of time. Truly, God is good!

By now it was the end of February (1996). But where would we go from here? Sadie was still too weak to return to our multilevel home in the mountains some miles from Boulder. In addition, she would need to continue her therapy on an outpatient basis. The rehabilitation center had a small cottage which might have been suitable, but it had been promised to some other guests. Renting an apartment in Boulder had little appeal; moreover, we doubted that we could find a suitable one.

We ultimately decided to go to the Desert Hot Springs Therapy Center, which is about fifty miles east of Loma Linda, California. Here, while still seated in her wheelchair, staff could transport Sadie into a pool of hot water and exercise her limbs. Following this, they treated her with hot packs and massage. She made such good progress that, although still confined to a wheelchair, we were able to fly back to Andrews University in Berrien Springs, Michigan, for her fiftieth anniversary reunion in late April. Since we were close to Battle Creek, we also made a return trip to the Battle Creek hospital. Needless to say, the hospital staff personnel were thrilled to see how much she had progressed.

Although initially Sadie had been an inpatient at Desert Hot Springs Therapy Center, she was anxious to move back into our trailer which I had parked in the adjoining parking lot. However, the trailer's floor sat approximately three feet above the ground level, Sadie couldn't manage the steps.

I found the solution to the problem in an unlikely place in the therapy center. To my amazement here sat a free-standing set of steps leading to a small platform. I had no idea about its original use or why it had been discarded. Although aged, it had been well-built with handrails on both sides. When the staff helped me put it in front of the trailer door, it was exactly the right height. The platform was big enough for a person to stand on and open the door. In addition, the height of each step was shorter than usual. Sadie could manage these! The design couldn't have been improved upon had it been specifically made for the purpose. Was this just another "accident?"

However, with that problem solved, additional trouble was brewing. While in the hospital and rehabilitation center, Sadie had been dependent upon tube feeding. The feeding tube had been removed because it irritated her. However, the trauma she had experienced extended to her digestive tract. It was becoming increasingly difficult for her to obtain adequate nutrition. By mid-May she was in serious trouble. She had no appetite, and the food she did manage to put down soon returned the same way. She was losing weight!

In what we believe was another of God's many providences, we were led to a specialist in central California who had done a considerable amount of research in this area. Actually, we knew him since he had spent some time in Boulder a decade or more earlier. His grandson had been one of Sadie's special students. However, we would never have thought of approaching him had not the staff of the therapy center suggested this doctor. Although the doctor no longer accepted new patients, when he heard of Sadie's problem, he agreed to see what he could do for her.

"Sadie has acute metabolic exhaustion, which is closely related to anorexia," the doctor told us. "Except for some people who have been terminally ill and in the last week of their lives, I have never seen anyone whose amino acid levels are so low."

Because of the trauma to Sadie's small intestine, it was severely limited in its ability to absorb and process the nutrients it needed to repair the damage to itself. Once again, Sadie was on the threshold of, if not immersed in, a life-threatening complication.

However, with God's blessing, and the help of some amino acids and other dietary supplements, Sadie slowly developed an appetite and regained some weight. By now it was mid-August; the daytime temperatures were 120°F or so. Our fifth wheel trailer was parked on black asphalt, and the air conditioner was running about twenty hours a day. Actually, all things considered, we were reasonably comfortable, but with the improvement in Sadie's condition, we decided to return to Colorado for a few months to assure ourselves that all was in order there. We anticipated returning to the therapy center in Southern California for the winter.

The return to Colorado was traumatic for Sadie. Including the months we had been gone prior to her accident, she had been away from home for more than a year. Following corrective surgery to her left wrist, we returned to Desert Hot Springs Therapy Center. We continued going to Desert Hot Springs during each winter.

Chapter 23

Perhaps the major setback came in April of 1998. As we were returning to our home in Colorado for the summer, we decided to go by Walla Walla, Washington, to visit some friends and relatives. About fifty miles short of Walla Walla, we paused at a rest stop. Here, upon exiting the trailer, one of Sadie's knees gave way and she fell three feet, landing on her side on the hard asphalt. She was unable to get up. Using a cell phone, I called 911 for help. An ambulance took her to a nearby hospital. Initially, the doctors thought she might have broken her hip, but no, her injury was far worse. Although the head or ball of the femur was intact, the force with which she had landed had shattered the mating socket in her pelvis.

In order to heal properly, a surgeon would first need to restore the pieces to their proper positions and give the bone a chance to knit. Following this, and because there would almost certainly be "irregularities" in the resulting socket, she would likely need a more or less standard "hip replacement." In terms of its difficulty, this initial procedure was reportedly second only to brain surgery. It was far beyond the training of the medical staff at the local hospital.

We called our friend and orthopedic surgeon in Boulder.

"No," he said, "I don't do that kind of surgery either. But I will see if I can find someone who does."

In a few days he called us. "There is a specialist in Denver who does that type of surgery. He is willing to accept Sadie as a patient."

It took several additional days to make the necessary arrangements. We went by air ambulance, this time by a Learjet, again courtesy of our insurance company. Upon arrival at the Denver hospital, the doctor obtained additional tests and x-rays. Finally, the surgery was scheduled but, at the appointed time, Sadie had developed a bladder infection. Another delay. By the time I finally bid her "farewell" and she was wheeled into the operating room, more than two weeks had elapsed since the accident.

An hour or so later, Sadie awoke to find herself in the recovery room. But something didn't seem just right. The pain she had been expecting wasn't there. She soon learned the rest of the story. After administering the anesthesia, but before making the incision, the surgeon had decided that he wanted to have one final "look" at the problem with which he would be dealing. He had ordered more x-rays. Upon looking at them, he did a double take: There was little he could do to improve the alignment of the different pieces; moreover, the bone had already started to knit! He sent Sadie directly to the recovery room.

The need for a major and difficult surgery had been averted!

As anticipated, however, in time she did need a hip replacement. Sadie came through the surgery with flying colors. The doctor removed the top portion of her femur which would be replaced with a prosthesis. The removed bone had been "ground up" and became part of a bone graft which added stability to her pelvis.

Following this, Sadie had two knee replacements. During the first of these, and following the incision which exposed the interior of her left knee, the operating team gasped, "How has that woman been able to stand on that leg, to say nothing of being able to walk?" Four months later she had the second knee replacement.

Epilogue

By 1999 it had been a decade or so since Sadie and I had last been in Denmark. Much had happened in the interim. Sadie was still in rehabilitation and only marginally able to travel. Aunt Emma, Anna, and Carla had all gone to their final rest. What a wonderful day that will be when we can be reunited with our loved ones in heaven!

For many years our son, David, had wanted to visit the place of his grandfather's birth. At last, we really could. He had provided the funds for the trip. Cousin Peter accompanied us as together we visited the church in Elling and the adjoining cemetery where Grandfather and other family members had been buried. We visited "Engen," the farm from which the name adopted by the children from Grandfather's first marriage had been taken.

On the last day of our eventful visit, we had visited an "open air" museum at Skagen, on the extreme northern tip of Denmark. I had been interested to learn that one of the windmills there on display had at one time been used on the Engen farm. Peter and I had been reminiscing about the past. Somewhere in his files, Peter had a biographical sketch which our grandfather had prepared, telling among other things of the "moat" which he had devised to protect his farm from the incursions of the Baltic Sea which adjoined his land. In addition to supervising the activities of his large farm, Grandfather had also served his country as a "*sognefoged*," whose role was somewhat similar to that of a "justice of the peace." Following World War I, and in recognition of his performance of the duties related therewith, Grandfather had been awarded the "Cross of the Order of Dannebrog"[25] by King Christian the Tenth. This decoration was established on the twelfth of October, 1671, by King Christian the Fifth. On the cross is engraved: *Gud og Kongen* [God and the King].

Although Danish law had required the return of the associated medal upon Grandfather's death, the family had been allowed to keep a small replica. If there was a family heirloom, this most certainly was it! For many years it had been treasured by Aunt Emma and, upon her death, it had been inherited by Peter. Many were the times I had paused to look at it during my visits to Aunt Emma.

The hour was late. Our conversation had just about run its course. In a few moments we would bid farewell. Peter excused himself for a few moments then reappeared. To my utter surprise he handed me the box containing the replica. "I am giving this to you," he said.

---

25   "*Dannebrog*" is the name of the Danish flag.

Apart from the initial shock, my immediate impulse was, of course, to refuse. What claim did I have on it? Why should I have it? He certainly had as much right to it as I did and probably much more. He had sons who one day would inherit it. But I didn't have a chance to say anything.

"I think it belongs on your side of the Atlantic," Peter continued. "All of our grandfather's children, except me, live there."

I then recognized that Peter's offer, to thus surrender a cherished possession, was not without personal pain or a sense of loss. However, I also realized that were I to refuse his offer, he would be genuinely hurt.

After I had expressed these ideas, I then accepted the offer with the understanding that it would not be considered "mine" in the usual sense of the word but rather that I would accept it as a custodian and on behalf of all of the grandchildren (Peter's cousins) on this side of the Atlantic.

As I have looked back, I cannot help but feel that there may have been a deeper significance to this transaction. To the best of my understanding and perception, whatever tension may have existed among the siblings from Grandfather's two marriages had never been passed on to the next generation, the one of which I am a part. Or if any fragment had slipped through, it had certainly vanished during the events recorded in this story. On the other hand, not that it was needed, but this transaction certainly brought a "closure" to whatever tensions may have existed between the members of the prior generation.

Postscript

I write these lines from Desert Hot Springs where Sadie and I continued to travel until 2009. Sadie continued her therapy and grew stronger every day. The major surgeries were all behind her; the life-threatening issues resolved in her favor. Her daily routine included a walk of a mile or more, without the benefit of even a cane. Truly, God has been good!

The experience of Sadie's accident was traumatic for both of us, but we faced the future with courage. We can never know what the future holds but we know He holds the future. May God bless each of you who are reading these lines; may this account have been a source of encouragement to you and may we all join hands in that "better land." This is my prayer for you.

****

Sadie Owen Engen passed to her rest in April 2009. She was a friend to all, a mentor to many, a supporter of those in crisis, and a much-loved substitute teacher. Certainly, she was an asset in this world, and many people look forward to seeing her in that "better land."

****

Glenn F. Engen passed to his rest in November 2022, while this book was in the process of being published. Three weeks before his death, he was able to proofread the book and correct some important details. He would want each reader to plan to meet him "in that better land."

TEACH Services, Inc.
P U B L I S H I N G

We invite you to view the complete
selection of titles we publish at:
www.TEACHServices.com

We encourage you to write us
with your thoughts about this,
or any other book we publish at:
info@TEACHServices.com

TEACH Services' titles may be purchased in
bulk quantities for educational, fund-raising,
business, or promotional use.
bulksales@TEACHServices.com

Finally, if you are interested in seeing
your own book in print, please contact us at:
publishing@TEACHServices.com
We are happy to review your manuscript at no charge.

www.ingramcontent.com/pod-product-compliance
Lightning Source LLC
Chambersburg PA
CBHW060441090426
42733CB00011B/2359